Hydroponics for beginners

*The Ultimate Guide with Strategies and Techniques
on How to Build Your Own Garden at Home*

BY: ALEX MOORE

©Copyright 2020 by Alex Moore

circumstances will any legal responsibility or blame be held against the publisher for any reparation, damages, or monetary loss due to the information herein, either directly or indirectly.

Respective authors own all copyrights not held by the publisher.

The information herein is offered for informational purposes solely and is universal as so. The presentation of the information is without a contract or any type of guarantee assurance. The trademarks that are used are without any consent, and the publication of the trademark is without permission or backing by the trademark owner. All trademarks and brands within this book are for clarifying purposes only and are owned by the owners themselves, not affiliated with this document.

Table of Contents

Introduction

Many first civilizations have utilized hydroponic developing strategies at some stage in history. The hanging gardens of Babylon, the floating gardens of the Aztecs of Mexico and people of the Chinese language are examples of 'Hydroponic' way of life. Egyptian hieroglyphic facts relationship back several hundred years B.C. describe the growing of plant life in water. At the same time as hydroponics is an ancient technique of developing plants, enormous strides had been made through the years on this innovative place of agriculture. Throughout the last century, scientists and horticulturists experimented with distinctive methods of hydroponics. One of the capability packages of hydroponics that drove studies turned into growing fresh produce in non-arable areas of the sector and regions with little to no soil. Hydroponics turned into used at some stage in global conflict II to deliver troops stationed on non-arable islands in the Pacific with fresh produce grown in regionally established hydroponic structures. Later in the century, hydroponics became included in the distance program.

As NASA considered the practicalities of locating a society on every other planet or the Earth's moon, hydroponics effortlessly fit into their sustainability plans. By way of the Seventies, it wasn't only scientists and analysts who have been worried about hydroponics. Conventional farmers and eager hobbyists started to be attracted to the virtues of hydroponic growing.

A FEW OF THE BENEFITS OF HYDROPONICS INCLUDE:

- The capacity to supply better yields than conventional, soil-based agriculture.

- It is permitting food to be grown and fed on in areas of the world that cannot aid crops in the soil.

- We are casting off the want for prominent pesticide use (thinking about maximum pests live within the soil), correctly making our air, water, soil, and meals cleanser.

Chapter 1

Equipment Required

Hydroponic gardening, or developing plants without soil, has been around for hundreds of years. It's only since the 1930s, but, that this shape of agriculture has come into enormous use among home gardeners. Hydroponic gardens may be very intricate; however, it's possible to construct an easy but effective "soil-less garden" with only some primary materials. A variety of hydroponic kits are to be had for purchase. Even as numerous methods of hydroponic gardening exist, all of them use equal fundamental equipment and resources. Hydroponic gardening, or developing plants without soil, has been around for heaps of years. It's most effective for the reason that the 1930s, but that this shape of agriculture has come into significant use amongst home gardeners. Hydroponic gardens can be challenging, but it's possible to build an easy but powerful "soil-less garden" with just a few primary materials. If you are interested in hydroponic gardening, you'll want to apply the best gadget to have any danger of fulfillment. Depending on your level of experience, to be had budget and gardening wishes, you may pick one of the many styles of hydroponic structures to be had. But, as you may word, a number of the crucial bits of equipment used to build exclusive systems are comparable. Selecting the satisfactory of simple hydroponics device, as decided through your precise gardening requirements, will assist make the paintings of excelling at hydroponics plenty easier? Quite several hydroponic kits are to be had for buy. Even as several strategies of hydroponic gardening exist, they all use the same essential device and components.

THE RESERVOIR

The reservoir utilized in hydroponic structures holds the water that, during the turn, contains the nutrients to be supplied on your plants. Because of the maximum simple issue of any hydroponic gadget, the reservoir holds the water that is hard to keep your plant awash with moisture and minerals. Relying on your finances as well as the scale of your operation, the reservoir may be something from a pricey business variation or an easy bucket. To prevent evaporation of the water held therein, which would affect the nutrient balance, make sure to pick a reservoir that includes a lid. Moreover, the satisfactory reservoir needs not to be metal as it can result in the advent of harmful minerals into the nutrient answer or the incidence of chemical reactions that can emerge as hurting your plant.

WATER PUMP

To deliver your plant with the water and minerals they need to live on, and you need to search out a dependable water pump. The two essential varieties of water pumps are submersible and non-submersible. The former is installed inside the nutrient answer even as the latter desires to be hooked up outside the solution. Water pumps also are categorized consistent with their output in Gallons per Minute (GPM) or Gallons, according to Hour (GPH). When you have a small installation, then a pump that supplies around 30 to 40 GPH could be able to provide your plants with the water they want, and gainers cost plenty.

Make sure to additionally recall the price at which water drains from the grow media when deciding on a water pump that meets the desired degree of output.

TIMER

In maximum hydroponic structures, except the most fundamental ones, a timer is required to help with the regulation of several essential capabilities. As an example, a timer may be used to adjust watering, ventilation, and lighting cycles. While deciding on the high-quality timer on your system, you may have predominant picks, less complicated and more affordable analog gadgets or costlier, other superior virtual devices. The later is first-rate for those seeking to create a gadget for developing sensitive plant life that requires utmost accuracy for the duration of the execution of every operation.

LIGHTING

To decorate the boom of your plants, you want to have the proper development lighting. It's miles critical to say at this point that although fluorescent lighting may be used to supplement natural light, they cannot, on their own, provide the spectrum of mild wanted via plants. Steel Halide and excessive stress Sodium lighting had been evolved to emit a spectrum of mild that mimics the satisfactory of mild emanating from the sun. Metal Halide lighting fixtures are the closest you could get to daylight. They produce extra a higher percentage of blue light that is remarkable for assisting vegetative growth. Excessive strain sodium lights then again produce mild that covers greater of the pink-orange spectrum. They were closing longer burn brighter and devour a lower quantity of energy than their steel halide opposite numbers, even though they produce a narrower spectrum of mild. For the excellent effects, it is recommended that you combine the use of both kinds of lighting fixtures to provide mild this is as near as possible to the whole spectrum of daylight. Furthermore, you can use mild reflectors and movers to cover a much wider space with fewer lighting fixtures.

GROWTH MEDIA

The soil has no location in hydroponics; inert, non-organic materials are utilized in its area. The increase in media is used to aid the plant because it grows. The medium chosen ought to, in addition to anchoring the plant, facilitate right drainage and aeration of the roots. Polyurethane foam, perlite, bark, gravel, vermiculite, and coconut fiber are several useful options right here. The proper increase medium should be dense sufficient to anchor the plant; however, no longer a lot that it hinders the circulate of air and the nutrient answer. The particles of the medium ought to be able to preserve moisture and nutrients long enough to permit the roots to absorb the necessary level of Nutrient among flooding. Ultimately it has to be sterile to save you the propagation of sicknesses, pests, and parasites.

PH TEST KIT

You want to maintain the pH stability of the nutrient solutions to have any danger of growing a wholesome hydroponic garden. Although a few plant life can be able to thrive at a decrease or better pH level, its miles advocated that you keep it at between 6 and 6.5. Which means you need to accumulate a pH test kit? Of the entire hydroponic gadget discussed above, those kits are the maximum cheap, but also most of the most vital. Growing a hydroponic garden includes less work than building a lawn inside the soil. However, to prevail, you want to have the nice hydroponics gadget from the beginning, irrespective of whether you pick out to go with a prepared-made kit or are planning on placing collectively your very own system step by step.

CONTAINER

No matter the technique used, all hydroponic gardens require some form of box or tank to keep the solution that gives nutrients to the plant life. Many homemade hydroponic gardens use a huge storage container, water trough, or even a kiddie's pool for a tank. The material used to make the tank isn't critical as long as it's far watertight and blocks out most of the light. A great rule of thumb is to have a box; this is between 6 and 18 inches deep and a couple of to a few feet across.

SUPPORTING PLATFORM/PLANT BED

A platform or plant mattress is essential to help the plant as they develop. Preferably, it should be large enough to absolute cowl the box. For water-way of life systems wherein the roots grow immediately inside the water, the plant life is positioned in holes in the platform and held in the region through cotton or comparable cloth packed across the stem. Homemade systems often use a thick piece of Styrofoam or the lid of the garage field because of the platform. For mixture-culture systems, the vegetation is positioned in a nonsoil growing media, also referred to as combination or muddle. The aggregate may be held in character mesh containers that can be placed within the supporting platform, or the platform may be a trough with a porous bottom. This is packed with aggregate. The nutrient solution is carried out to the combination so it could are available in contact with the roots.

AGGREGATE

An extensive type of substance can be used as a hydroponic combination. Alternatives include sand, gravel, vermiculite, timber shavings, peat moss, perlite, and a fibrous stone fabric referred to as Rockwool. The secret's that or not it's inert, offering no nutrients to the plant. It should also be strong sufficient to appropriately guide the plant as they grow and be at least 3 inches intensive.

NUTRIENT SOLUTION

The entire Nutrient needed for a plant to grow in a hydroponic device has to be provided via the nutrient solution. A number of the nutrients that need to be a gift within the answer are nitrogen, phosphorus, potassium, calcium, magnesium, sulfur, iron, and copper. Given the wide industrial availability of premixed nutrient solutions, it's far more comfortable and generally more effective to apply those than to try to prepare homemade solutions.

AERATION

Further to Nutrient, the plant wants to draw oxygen into its roots to live on. Meaning some technique of aeration is vital to make sure there is sufficient oxygen within the nutrient solution. For smaller gardens, this can be performed through emptying and refilling the container with an answer. Larger systems regularly use an air bubbler, similar to those located in aquariums, to keep the nutrient answer oxygenated.

LIGHT

Hydroponic gardens may be grown interior or outside. Because vegetation, particularly greens, need lots of mild to thrive, an artificial light source can be wished for an indoor lawn. Fluorescent or incandescent bulbs may be used as long as they offer enough quantity of mild from the pink and blue variety of the mild visible spectrum.

CONSIDERATIONS FOR PURCHASING YOUR HYDROPONICS EQUIPMENT

Coming into the arena of hydroponics could be very amusing and enjoyable; however, it could also be extremely intimidating. There are such a lot of options for getting your hydroponics gadget that it can sense overwhelming. At the same time, as it can be tempting to buy the first gadget that appears cheap and clean to use to you, you don't need to wind up with a wa system that doesn't shape your needs. Here are the most critical factors consider while buying your gadget.

You're Available Space

– In which precisely will you be developing your plant? A small greenhouse for your outdoor? A large closet? Your basement? Earlier than you purchase your device, make sure which you calculate the rectangular pictures of the space you will be using and figure out exactly how plenty of hydroponics system you may install there. In case you are planning on developing rows of plants, attempt to allow at least one meter of the walking area among each row to make it simpler to tend on your lawn.

You're Plants –

You probably already have an idea of what you need to grow hydroponically. Now you need to ensure which you find hydroponics device, which can assist the ones in planting life grow their ability. You don't want to purchase small, shallow trays if your plant life has more extensive, thick roots. And you don't need to waste your cash on numerous eighteen-inch buckets if all you need to develop is smaller plant life. Talk in your hydroponics retailer approximately what form of device, medium, and fertilizer could excellent accommodate the dimensions and developing fee of your plant life. Many producers additionally have telephone numbers that permit you to speak to hydroponics professionals about these styles of growing troubles.

You're Budget –

Before you buy your hydroponics gadget, you should decide upon how much money you are willing to spend, and try and make absolutely the excellent use of those finances. It is essential to preserve in mind, but that start-up prices aren't the most straightforward expense associated with hydroponics. You need to additionally try to factor in how a good deal power your lights would require and how regularly you can have to update your device. If you plan on maintaining your hydroponics system for years, it could prevent quite a few cash from spending a touch extra while you genuinely purchase the system.

You're Time –

Like most interest growers, you probably don't need to devote all your time to developing your plant life. That is why you ought to recall precisely how hard work-intensive individuals systems are additionally. Something like an aeroponics gadget might appear at once attractive. However, for the reason that anything that is going incorrect with the timer might bring about a very brief drying out of the roots, those sorts of systems can sometimes require extra interest than maximum. The majority genuinely don't have the luxury of rushing from paintings to their home to keep their plant in the event of an electricity outage. So look for a machine that offers you a more considerable margin of error, inclusive of one that incorporates a medium that holds an excellent deal of air and water nicely.

Chapter 2

How To Get The Best Germination Rates

Hydroponic Germination Dos And Don'ts

If your germination chamber reaches intense temperatures on either aspect of the spectrum, you'll not get excellent germination prices, if any. Do no longer permit your seeds or media to dry out. Your seeds want to be heat and moist on the way to germinate, and forgetting to accomplish that, or permitting those to get too dry between watering will probably kill them. Maintaining your germination chamber at a higher humidity will assist reduce the chance of drying out as well as watering frequency? The usage of a humidity dome can assist the chamber in producing its very own humidity. Seeds and seedlings also can be too wet. In this example, the seed usually rots before it has a hazard to develop. You'll realize your media is too wet if it's soggy or falling aside. It needs to be pretty moist, but you need to see no water pooling in the tray for prolonged quantities of time.

TIPS FOR SUCCESSFUL HYDROPONIC PROPAGATION

At some stage in the seedling degree, plants are touchier to warmness. Even vegetation that selects warmer temperatures shouldn't be overexposed to heat in this stage. Seedlings are pretty sensitive all round so that you shouldn't be including too many nutrients, fertilizers, or pesticides. You can use a seedling heat mat to help preserve a perfect temperature on your propagation chamber. Continually retaining your media wet enough to be soggy can result in what's referred to as damping off. It can be resulting from a variety of molds and fungi, and in the propagation degree, reasons plants to lose stem structure and layover lat. We do endorse adding nutrients; however, not till after you see the initial set of real leaves. Use the identical nutrient blend as you will in develop-out, however, dilute it much also. You have to have an EC.Eight–1.2 as an absolute most. Keep in mind that all of the Nutrient a plant wishes in its first level of existence are supplied by way of the cotyledons. As soon as actual leaves show up, the plant will depend more on outside sources like soil or synthetic fertilizers.

GARDENING TIPS TO IMPROVE SEED GERMINATION

While you start vegetation from seeds, one of the maximum important stuff you want to attain is a very high and speedy germination rate. However, if you try to do seed germination with none extra effort, you will maximum likely achieve sub-most relevant results on account that some natural elements hinder seed germination that wants to be eliminated that allows you to reap the tremendous feasible results. A number of the maximum essential ranges in the growth of lawn greens is seed germination. Germination is how a seed grows into a new plant. There are plenty of variables that could come into play during seed germination, and in flip, a lot of factors that could cross incorrect. Consequently, educating yourself on the crucial factors affecting this process can help ensure a successful garden. Whether or not you are the usage of your heirloom seeds or purchasing seeds from a garden save, germination is going to be instead depending on environmental conditions. If you haven't had good fortune germinating many of your seeds inside the past, it could be due to mild, warmth, moisture, or a spread of other issues. Right here are some simple gardening guidelines for purchasing better, faster germination for all types of seeds.

1. PRE-SOAK YOUR SEEDS BEFORE PLANTING

Plants lie dormant until the seeds stumble on sufficient ordinary moisture to grow. That is why many seeds take a long time to germinate. You may "trick" the seed into commencing faster by way of pre-soaking them in water. The aim is to penetrate the outer floor of the shell so that the plant gets the sign that it's equipped to develop. Make sure you're planting the seeds at a suitable time of 12 months for the place you live in for the high-quality yield. Seed packets may also have the best planting instances indexed at the package deal, or you could test a seed planting calendar online.

2. BEGIN BY STARTING YOUR SEEDS INDOORS

If you're failing to germinate seeds outside, starting them interior can help. Purchase a seed tray and plant some seeds in each one. After your seedlings have grown, you may then flow them outside to continue to expand. This saves your plant in the course of their maximum prone period and helps you to control the quantity of water they get completed. Inside the new degrees of growth, a single hurricane should wipe out your new plant!

There's best one trap: if you begin your seeds inner, you need to harden them earlier than planting them outdoor. Which means slowly acclimating them to outdoor surroundings before being planted, starting with one or hours out of doors a day. And bear in mind, many plants are undoubtedly suitable to an indoor lawn. Herbs and some veggies may be grown quite luckily inside or in pots -- so you do not necessarily want to transport your plants outdoor.

3. MONITOR YOUR SEED'S ENVIRONMENT

Soil temperature sensors are ideal for growing seeds and seedlings to monitor soil conditions and make sure your plant stays inside the best temperatures, whether or not outdoor or indoors. Some indoor soil temperature sensors also can measure room temperature and humidity to offer even more information about growing conditions. Temperature is very vital because the seed wishes to "recognize" that the bloodless season is done and that it is time to develop. As much as they want moisture, seeds also need a steady warm temperature. Outside, this may commonly be delivered by direct daylight. Interior, you need for you to control the temperature. This additionally means that you'll want to keep your seeds in an area that is warm and well-lit. In the early days of your seedlings, they will not want much direct light -- but they may nonetheless want a few daylights. You could also put money into UV lamps as a way to have a twin purpose of each offering extra mild for your seedlings and also making them hotter. Maximum seedlings decide on temperatures, which might be among 60 to 70 tiers. If you acquire a seed packet, it can kingdom the ideal temperatures for the seed at the container. In any other case, you may test an internet soil temperature chart for the seeds you are planting.

4. KEEP THEM WELL-WATERED

As soon as your seeds were located and you have begun tracking lawn temperatures, you need to maintain them nicely-watered until they germinate. Too little moisture and the seeds may not germinate; too much moisture and they may begin to rot instead of developing. Some seeds take a long term to grow first of all. Lavender, for instance, can take anywhere from 4 to six weeks to germinate. For the duration of this time, face up to the urge to attempt to check on the seeds or disturb the oil. Instead, hold watering as wished and monitoring your sensors.

5. CHANGE SEED SOURCES

If your seeds have did not germinate, even given the above suggestions, it is entirely feasible the seeds themselves were duds. If seeds weren't stored nicely -- they may be left in a hot mailbox, as an instance -- they may sincerely now not be capable of germinating. If seeds had been saved in a frigid region, they'd be taking a while to "wake" up. And there are a few seeds that sincerely can't germinate; many seeds that are culled from grocery store vegetables and herbs, as an instance, are in no way going to grow. Then again, if seeds from multiple sources are failing to germinate, you can need to investigate both your soil and your water. Your potting soil won't have sufficient moisture absorption or drainage, or your water can also want to be filtered. You may also be in an environment that is too cold for seeds to germinate correctly, in which case you can need to spend money on something to warm the soil.

Recollect:

seeds "determine" to germinate while situations are suitable for plant boom. Meaning the most crucial thing in the course of the germination process is consistency in each temperature and moisture. Through making an investment in a few easy garden tools and coping with and tracking the surroundings, you ought to be able to massively enhance your germination charges -- and develop healthier plants overall.

TEMPERATURE IS CRITICAL.

While doing seed germination, one of the most critical factors is seed temperature. Some plant requires cold temperatures to germinate - as, for instance, spinach's germination rate drops to approximately 1/2 while you go from 15 to 25°C - even as other plants require higher temperatures - for coriander, it is the other. For your seedling emergence rate to be as excessive as viable, make sure which you are giving them the temperature they preferably want, which depends on the plant species.

Pretreat seeds with PEG-6000. Polyethylene glycol treatments can dramatically boom seed germination costs (see right here). We've got recognized this because the mid-1970's and we've additionally acknowledged that the most appropriate remedy period and air-drying outcomes alternate in line with plant species. Making use of general PEG-6000 treatment, as an, I defined here some years ago, might or might not paintings depending on the plant you are seeking to pictures with. For excellent outcomes, you need to search the scientific literature for the best PEG-6000 remedy or - if this record isn't always present - design your very own experiments for parenting this out.

SEED DISINFECTION

Seeds are typically blanketed in microorganisms that could significantly impair seed germination rates. That allows you to put off this difficulty seeds need to be disinfected previous to germination with a chemical agent (most commonly both hydrogen peroxide and sodium hypochlorite answers). For this purpose, answers inside the order of 0.1-2%, NaClO is widely used with distinctive soaking instances various among extraordinary papers. You can read extra about this sort of method here. Treatments are usually brief with disinfection lasting only a few mins with next plain water baths to get rid of any excess oxidant.

Chapter 3

Learn How To Become A Master At Cloning

You will have skilled plant re-growing missing elements whenever you have got pruned or topped your personal plant life. Pruning creates pressure for the plant that triggers a hormonal reaction, primarily to a flurry of the recent boom. Cloning is commonly done via taking cuttings. A small part of stem and leaf is reducing from the mother plant; then, the cut stem is dipped in a rooting hormone – typically a powder or gel – and grown on.

HOW TO CLONE WITH CUTTINGS

Cloning is some distance less complicated than you would possibly suppose, and its miles as relevant to the small-scale gardener cultivating four vegetation for him- or herself as it is for the industrial grower with 50 lighting fixtures. First, choose the plant you want to clone. The plant needs to be inappropriate fitness and free from pest infestation or sickness. If you choose an unhealthy plant to clone from, you're screwed from the start! Remember the fact that clones taken from a diseased plant will be wearing the same sickness as the mother. As soon as you have decided on your plant, search for areas of the recent increase. New growth is the first-rate for cloning because it tends to be softer and much less 'woody,' and so should root quicker – although any healthy stem with more than one leaf unit will work. Also, ensure that the mom plant is well hydrated, as vegetation which can be dry will no longer yield a wholesome cutting. Another vital component is the degree of growth. While you are taking a reduction, that reduction is at the precise identical stage of the plant life cycle because the mom plant it becomes taken from.

In case you reduce from a flowering plant, then that slicing is within the flowering degree and will preserve to flower! It's viable to interchange the plant again to the vegetative level through growing it under 18 hours of light (or preferably greater); however, this could stress the plant and lead to boom issues.

It is a whole lot higher to take cuttings from plants inside the vegetative stage before they are switched to flowering or, even better, maintain a mom plant in a perpetual nation of plants and use this as your supply of clones.

Don't take cuttings from, or try and clone, an auto-flowering plant; it'll be flowering as it roots out, which reasons developmental issues and – higher importantly – it could yield very little. One of the maximum crucial elements in taking cuttings is hygiene.

A brand new reducing is susceptible to pathogens getting into via the open tissue at the bottom of the stem. Using dirty equipment or operating in dirty surroundings is a surefire way of introducing fungal or bacterial pathogens in your clones. Make sure that you spend a further short while cleansing your reducing equipment and reducing area, and you will be rewarded with healthy cuttings that root speedy.

If you are using a growing medium inclusive of soil, cocos, or rock wool to raise clones, then it is essential to keep the correct stages of moisture in the medium and humidity within the air. Use some shape of a propagator, although it's merely small plastic bags positioned over every plant. A heated propagator with a lid is satisfactory as the warmth stimulates root growth, and the cover keeps humidity and stops the medium from drying out. Use the vents within the cover to ensure that the environment isn't too moist as this can motive rot or 'damping off.' It's miles a balancing act, but deliver it a few attempts, and also you'll master it!

Hydroponic cloning machines maintain the moisture balance for you and take out some of the guesswork. They involve putting the cuttings into neoprene collars, after which into small baskets that are suspended above a nutrient tank. The stems are misted with the nutrient answer and root out faster than in traditional propagation techniques. You can store yourself 3 to 5 days the usage of a cloning device. They could make variety in length from areas for some clones to over a hundred, and the better ones in the marketplace include a lid.

HOW TO KEEP A MOTHER PLANT

Retaining a mom plant is relatively cheaper and straightforward. A well-tended mother can be saved for multiple years if dealt with efficaciously.

Hold a separate mother room: mom plants need to be stored inside the vegetative stage of a boom on 18 hours (or even 20 hours) of light; this indicates they'll want to be kept out of the flowering room. Grow tents are a notable choice as several plants can be stored in mild-tight surroundings close to, or maybe inside, your essential room.

Pick the correct lighting:

Plant lighting that is at the blue end of the spectrum encourages vegetative boom, so if the usage of a concealed lighting fixtures gadget picks out a steel halide bulb. In case you're best retaining one or two mom plant, a blue CFL lamp or large T5 propagation lamp could be extra than good enough and will reduce down on heat.

Pick the perfect growing media:

You could preserve a mom for a long time in case you want, but long term plant will need a healthy root zone. If you need at hand-water, choose a mild and aerated medium that won't compact over the years – consisting of cocos or a mild potting soil. If you wish to use a hydroponic machine, cross for one, which allows you to use inert clay pebbles – adrip-feed gadget or 'ebb and float.' This could make sure that there may be plenty of oxygen across the roots.

Choose the suitable feed: A nitrogen-rich development formulation might be required as your base nutrient. Make sure you operate an enzyme product periodically to break down antique roots and maintain the foundation quarter smooth.

CLONING TOP TIPS

If the usage of a mom plant provides it an excellent spray with a nitrogen-based foliar feed, one or weeks before you're because of taking your cuttings. This will ensure that there may be lots of wholesome, new growth from which to select your clones. Preserve your cloning area separate from your essential growing location. This can save you any airborne pathogens present in the vital room from coming into your new clones. Remember the fact that healthy, mature plant life may not display any sign of ailment. However, pathogens may nevertheless be a gift.

Prep your vicinity: you'll need a pointy scalpel or razor blade, a box of water at pH five.Five – 6, rooting hormone, a comfortable mat, and your propagation medium or cloning system.

Take your cuttings: pick out a 3" or 4" stem complete with a few leaves; cut just underneath wherein the leaves be part of the stem (this 'internode' is in which your clone will produce roots) and area the reducing into the container of water. Repeat till you have got all of your cuttings.

Slice off the lower leaves wherein they join the stem and depart some leaves on the top of the reducing. Remember that the leaves require power to hold them, and also you want most of the people of the cuttings' energy to enter root increase. So, if the leaves at the cutting are quite massive, reduce off the end, about midway down the leaf. Much less leaf place requires less electricity to maintain it. Use a scalpel or razor blade to cut the bottom of the stem diagonally, ensuring the blade could be very sharp – this can keep away from crushing the stem. Dip the stem in rooting hormone. Usually, pour a quantity of powder or gel into a small box (or lid) to dip the cuttings. Don't dip into the first box, or you may contaminate your whole supply of hormone. Throw any excess gel or powder away; do not pour it lower back into the main container. Lightly slide, you are reducing into its propagation medium and place it right into a propagator. Roots will expand with 3 to seven days. If the use of a cloning device slips the reducing into the neoprene collar and turn on the pump, do no longer add nutrients to the reservoir until you see the first signs of root development, usually after three to five days. So, there you have it – cloning is a clean manner to ensure your crop is wholesome, develops at the same tempo, and is ready to reap at the same time. Plus, it's accurate amusing! Happy cloning!

HOW TO GET THE MOST OUT OF YOUR MOTHER PLANT

Rest assures beginner growers. Cloning isn't as tight as you would possibly assume it to be. That's the message Danny Sloat, grows expert and founder of cannabis cultivator AlpinStash, and desires to get throughout. For the uninitiated, cloning is while you're taking a clipping off a mother plant and root it. The clone — or reducing as it's every so often acknowledged — then grow into some other woman plant, and is a genetically similar clone to that authentic plant. Seeds, then again, come from a phenotype. When you start from seed, every seed of the same strain is ann exceptional phenotype — that is, an expression of the genetic trends, such as its taste, effectiveness, and look — which Sloat likens to siblings from identical parents. One sibling's genetics may lean in the direction of the father, the alternative may lean toward the mother, and however, they arrive from the same supply. "if you plant five seeds, all five of those seeds might be identical however extra than possibly they'll be special from every different," he explains. When cloning, however, you're developing the same plant as the only it was cut from.

Here are some essential dos and don'ts for beginner growers when it comes to cloning.

1. Do pick a healthful mom Plant

The healthier your mother plant is, the healthier your clone may be. A wholesome plant thrives, isn't mild inexperienced in the shade, but isn't exceptional dark either, and not using a purpling in the stem (until that is a genetic trait). It additionally shouldn't have drooping leaves or stem damage.

2. DO USE A GROW MEDIA?

The grow media you operate is the muse that offers your cutting something to root into so you can plant it. Your grow media will be soilless media, like coco coir or perlite, but Sloat prefers to use a spongy, compressed plug that works a great deal inside the similar way. He indicates soaking the media in a premixed beneficial bacteria and aloe water answer before putting the cutting in it. Then, vicinity the press under a dome, which is an included flower-mattress tray that maintains humidity while allowing mild to penetrate. Fantastic sprouted does a tremendous dome package that consists of fluorescent grow mild and warmth mat.

3. DO USE A ROOTING GEL

Premade gels don't require mixing with water and are a convenient manner of giving your plant life the variety of hormones they want to encourage rooting growth. "Not handiest do [rooting gel] supply hormones, but it also assists seal the cut you make," Sloat says. The primary danger while cloning is that exposed cuts will suck up air, which could result in an embolism — a blockage within the form of an air bubble an excellent way to save you water and Nutrient from transferring up the plant, inflicting them to die. But, in case you dip the reduction in gel, it'll seal and prevent the air embolism, at the same time as imparting the hormones that encourage rooting. Please note that at the same time as premade rooting gels are handy, due to the fact they're premade, you received to be able to adjust concentration levels.

4. DON'T PERMIT YOUR CLONE TO TAKE A SEAT OUTDOOR FOR TOO LONG

In case you make a reduce, and aren't immediately going to plant it, you have to submerge it in water. Don't leave it bare inside the open, or it'll die. You can leave it within the water for up to two weeks, at the same time as a few experienced growers suggest that you could keep clones which have been immersed in water in a zipper-lock bag, and region them within the non-freezer a part of a fridge to preserve them for up to six weeks.

5. DON'T FERTILIZE THE WATER YOU'RE USING

While weed loves food, and you can damage your clones in case you're too beneficent with the fertilizer after they're trying to root. This is due to the fact some of the Nutrient in plant meals, like nitrogen, inspire the plant life to cultivate new boom on the tip and discourage rooting, at the same time as others can be negative to rooting. Sloat admits that for the first to three weeks, he uses little more than faucet or spring water for his cloned vegetation. "I don't use something fancy on [them]."However, as soon as transplanted, you may steadily introduce fertilizer into their diet.

6. DO MAKE SURE YOUR CLONES HAVE NODES OF ENERGETIC INCREASE

Other than looking for evidence of two nodes, which are the regions from which leaves grow, your clone should have at least one to two nodes below that growing tip. Sloat says about four–6 inches tall ought to be enough. You want to reduce a forty-five-degree attitude, so there's extra floor location for the roots to grow from.

7. DO HOLD YOUR DEVELOP MEDIA WET

Preserve it moist, however, now not soaking, all through the system. Ensure there's moisture inside the dome by way of spraying the leaves a few times an afternoon. Sloat suggests the use of a heating mat to help the water evaporate.

8. DO PERMIT YOUR CLONE TO HARDEN OFF AS SOON AS THE PLANT STARTS EVOLVED TO ROOT

Hardening off is while you intentionally and lightly reveal plants that have been grown indoors to the factors out of doors in a bid to toughen them up. This helps save you transplant shock, which can lead to stunted or lifeless seedlings because of the unexpected adjustments in temperature. In case you're the use of a humidity dome, hardening is while you put off the humidity but keep the medium moist, so the plant life adapts to an environment that doesn't have eighty or one hundred percent humidity. In case you're using a humidity dome, open the holes on the top to set free the moisture. Ultimately you may take the dome off altogether. If you're an experienced grower who needs more in-intensity cloning advice, examine our posts on shopping for and delivery marijuana clones and clone-most useful traces.

FACTORS SHOULD YOU CONSIDER WHEN CHOOSING A SYSTEM?

Aside from ease of use and margin of errors, you also need to remember numerous factors so one can affect your desire.

SPACE

Typically, a small hydroponic system calls for around 16 square feet of floor space. Of direction, the dimensions of your machine will even depend on the number of flora you need to develop. Make sure that the system you're looking at will stay effortlessly healthy within the space you're making plans on putting it up.

AUTOMATION

You want to make sure that the temperature of your solution, the lights, humidity, and the water levels of your system are maintained at the first tiers. Things are, in reality, less complicated if you use an automated device, so you may additionally want to remember shopping for one that already has that feature.

EXPANDABILITY

You could choose to start small, mainly if you're best starting your hydroponics journey. However, once you get a taste of achievement, you may want to get a hold of the more magnificent plant to grow. Other than wanting a new area, you can need to look for a hydroponic device that's without difficulty expandable to deal with more vegetation. Otherwise, you could buy a brand new machine and start from 0 all yet again.

ENERGY EFFICIENCY

You'll be making use of strength to both pump water or air into your system. Because of this, you'll need to make sure which you get a gadget that is energy green.

SETUP COSTS

Some systems may be bought pre-constructed that could save you money and time ultimately. DIY tasks or those who require expert help while putting in place will require you to pay extra money. Both to get an expert to build it for you or to restoration a mistake you made in constructing your machine.

Chapter 4

The Basic Hydroponic System Types

How hydroponic systems work might also appear complicated in the beginning, but when you understand them, you'll see how they work sincerely virtually pretty efficiently. There are six sorts of hydroponic structures (Drip system, Ebb & waft, N.F.T., Water subculture, Aeroponics, and Wick). The vegetation roots want three things, water/moisture, Nutrient, and oxygen. What makes the six sorts of hydroponic systems extraordinary is really how they supply those three matters to the plants' roots. Each kind of system is defined within the element inside the hyperlinks (by name) to the left and beneath. Regardless of what they'll pick out to name them, all hydroponic systems are based totally on these six sorts and are either this kind of type of structure or a combination of two or more of the six types. There are lots of ways to make variations, also, to alter any issue of any of the six types of structures. So as soon as you're acquainted with how every of the three roots desires (water, Nutrient, and oxygen) are delivered in every type of hydroponic machine, you'll fast be able to pick out what kind of device any hydroponic gadget is.

- N F T hydroponic system The Six Types of Hydroponic Systems

- Drip System

- Ebb- Flow (Flood & Drain)

- N.F.T. (Nutrient Film Technique)

- Water Culture

- Aeroponics

- Wick System

WHAT ABOUT AQUAPONICS?

A few may additionally argue that aquaponics is another type of hydroponic gadget. However, aquaponics is not merely the 7th form of hydroponic device, simply because what makes aquaponics specific is how the Nutrient is formulated. No longer how the nutrients (or maybe water and oxygen) are delivered to the root, the technique of aquaponics and offering the nutrients from decomposing fish waste can be utilized in any of the six styles of hydroponic systems, actually using changing the natural nutrient reservoir with a fish tank reservoir. There's plenty more significant to aquaponics than that because you're looking to control different nutrient stages obviously with microorganisms, bacteria, and micro vegetation living inside the fish water to decompose the fish waste into the nutrients the plants can use. Without a doubt placed, aquaponics is a manner of creating Nutrient out of fish waste; basically, you're making your Nutrient. But that doesn't affect how water, nutrients, or oxygen are brought to the plant roots.

HYDROPONIC DRIP SYSTEMS

Drip systems are one of the maxima broadly used sorts of hydroponic structures around the world, each for home growers in addition to business growers alike. This is mainly as it's an easy concept and desires a few elements, but it's a flexible and effective type of hydroponic system. Although it's a neat concept, it may not restrict your creativeness when constructing your systems. The way a drip system works is similar to its sounds, and you certainly drip nutrient solution on the plant roots to keep them moist.

Hydroponic Drip SystemHydroponic drip systems can efficiently be designed in many methods, in addition to from small to massive structures. But they're especially useful for more extensive vegetation that takes a variety of root space. It is due to the fact you don't want vast volumes of water to flood the system, and the drip traces are smooth to run over more extended areas. In addition to when the usage of a larger quantity of growing media for large plants, more significant developing media retains more moisture than smaller amounts, and that's especially beneficial to dense vegetation as it's more forgiving to the plants.

EBB & FLOW - (FLOOD AND DRAIN) SYSTEM

Flood and Drain (Ebb and waft) systems are very popular with domestic hydroponic growers for lots of reasons. Except how smooth they're for everybody to build, you could use nearly any materials you have laying round to construct them with so that you don't want to spend much cash on growing plant life hydroponically. Additionally, they can be built to healthy in any available space you would possibly have (each indoors or outside), and there's no restriction to the distinct and imaginative methods to design them for that space. Together with being less expensive and clean to build, plants develop thoroughly in flood and drain systems. The flood and drain system works necessarily love it sounds, through clearly flooding the vegetation root device with nutrient solution. Most effective periodically rather than continuously. How a hydroponic flood and drain device operates quite simple. The original part of the flood and drain machine holds the containers the plant is developing in. It can be just one plant or many vegetation/packing containers in series. A timer turns on the pump, and water (nutrient answer) is pumped through tubing from the reservoir up into the first part of the device the usage of a submersible fountain/pond pump. The nutrient solution maintains to fill (flood) the machine until it reaches the peak of the preset overflow tube so that it soaks the vegetation roots. The overflow tube has to be set to approximately 2 inches underneath the pinnacle of the developing media.

While the water filling/flooding, the gadget reaches the overflow tube height. It drains back off to the reservoir where it recirculates again via the device. The overflow tube sets the water level top inside the flood and drains gadget, as well as makes sure the water (nutrient solution) would not spill out the pinnacle of the machine while the pump is on. When the pump shuts off, the water siphons go into reverse into the reservoir through the pump (draining the device).

THERE ARE THREE MAIN TYPES OF FLOOD AND DRAIN SYSTEM SETUPS

Plant containers in series design

This kind of structure is most usually used, while many exceptional boxes with plants are being watered (flooded) at the identical time. It is essential to keep in mind that the machine with Ebb&flow Flood and drain systems the plant (packing containers) to be flooded (watered) desires to be above the reservoir, like on a tabletop or bench. That ma,nner, the water can waft lower back to the reservoir by using natural gravity, and as a consequence,ence drain the device efficaciously. First, multiple packing containers are all linked collectively via tubing so that once the gadget is flooded, all of them flood flippantly, and all at the identical time. For simplicity, instead of getting a separate overflow for every container being flooded, there's usually the most straightforward one overflow tube. It connects to the machine at the bottom, wherein all the packing containers are related to. And when the water peak reaches the top of the overflow, it spills over Ebb&float Flood and drains the system and is going back to the reservoir to be pumped through the system again. The height of this one overflow tube will set the peak of the water level in all of the related bins with the plant life in them (as long because it's a stage). You could trade the water top in all of the linked containers by using adjusting the peak of the single overflow tube.

Flooding tray design

The flooding desk/tray flood and drain (ebb and flow) machine type setup are beneficial while you want to place the plant in the device briefly, need to be transferring them around a lot, or Ebb&drift Flood and drain table design starting plants to be positioned in another large machine. In place of flooding separate bins with plant life in it, this technique only overflows one container. Usually, a shallow rectangular or rectangle box that sets on the pinnacle of a table.

The reservoir typically sits immediately below with easy access. Ebb&float Flood and drain desk when flooded Water is pumped up from the reservoir into the flooding tray on one aspect and the overflow is on the other aspect of the flooding tray. That makes positive the water, in reality, circulates from one aspect of the tray/desk to the opposite. Like several flood and drain (ebb and glide) machine, the overflow tube peak units the water height for the duration of the flooding cycle, and may be adjusted as needed. Ebb&float Flood and drain table while drained

The plants are grown in ordinary plastic pots or baskets

and located inside the flooding tray like an everyday potted plant. However, not like an ordinary potted plant, hydroponic developing media is used for potting the plant as opposed to using potting soil. As soon as the plant gets massive sufficient, it can be transferred right into an everlasting hydroponic machine.

One drawback to the use of the flooding desk is the algae increase, and need to be cleaned out regularly. Due to the fact, the pinnacle of the tray is typically left open, and light is permitted to get into the nutrient answer within the bottom of the tray, which allows algae to grow. The algae by myself aren't sincerely bad for the plants, but it does burn up dissolved oxygen inside the water.

Serge tank flood and drain (ebb and flow) system design

The surge tank form of flood and drain setup is useful while extra vertical area is needed. Usually, with flood and drain systems, the reservoir are always decrease than the hydroponic Ebb flow Flood and drain structures with serge tank system. It's so the water (nutrient answer) can drain out of the gadget via gravity lower back into the reservoir via the overflow, and while the pump is off. However, you may nevertheless installation a flood and drain machine even if the water stage in the reservoir is better than the hydroponic system it's supposed to flood and drain again from. That is with the use of a surge tank. The surge tank form of flood and drain device expenses extra to construct because there are numerous more significant elements wanted. It works at the main Ebb glide Flood and drain systems with surge tank in the flooding cycle that water seeks its stage. In other words, the water height in one box will be equal in any other field while they're related below the waterline. The surge tank serves as a temporary reservoir that controls the water height in all of the packing containers with the plant life in them and is most effective complete at some point in the flooding cycle. Ebb flow Flood and drain systems with surge tank in flooding cycle The surge tank flood and drain (ebb and drift) device operates by using pumping water (nutrient solution) from the a good deal larger principal reservoir into the serge tank while the pump timer is going on. As the water stage rises in the serge tank, the water degree rises frivolously in all of the linked plant bins on equal time. While the water level gets excessive enough, a float valve in the Ebb flow Flood and drain structures with a surge tank in the drain cycle surge tank turns on a pump inside the surge tank. The pump within the serge tank then pumps water back into the primary reservoir. Right, now, each of the pumps is on (pump in first reservoir and surge tank). After the timer for the pump in the major reservoir shuts off, the pump inside the serge tank remains on. The pump in the serge tank maintains pumping all the water again into the principle reservoir (draining the machine) until the water level receives low enough. At that factor, a 2nd drift valve shuts off the pump inside the surge tank.

N.F.T. (NUTRIENT FILM TECHNIQUE) SYSTEM

The N.F.T. System (Nutrient movie technique) is pretty popular with home hydroponic growers as properly. Especially because its a fairly easy layout. But N.F.T. Systems are satisfactory ideal for, and maximum normally used for developing smaller short growing plant life like specific sorts of lettuce. Together with developing lettuce, some industrial growers also grow specific varieties of herbs and toddler vegetables, the usage of N.F.T. Structures. Even as there are lots of specific approaches to design for an N.F.T. Device, all of them have the same characteristic of a shallow nutrient solution, hydroponic n.F.T. Systemcascading downward through the tubing. Where the naked roots of the plant come in touch with the water and might take in the nutrients from it. The main downside to an N.F.T. Structures is that the vegetation is very sensitive to interruptions within the glide of water from power outages (or whatever reason). The plant life will start to wilt very quickly any time the water stops flowing through the device.

N.F.T. SYSTEM FLOW RATE, AND CHANNEL SLOPE

How deep should the water be, and the manner rapid have to the water be flowing are the two maximum commonplace questions requested approximately this type of machine. First, the slope of the channel controls how speedy the water goes through the tube/channel (not the water pump or).

The encouraged slope for an N.F.T. Device is commonly a 1:30 to 1: 40 ratio. That is for each 30 to forty inches of the horizontal period; one inch of drop (slope) is commonly encouraged. We endorse even as designing your N.F.T. Systems, you layout it so you can alter the slope while the plants are although developing. It is because of the truth as the idea structures get larger, they will cause it to pool and dam up the water flow. If it's miles adjust, able, you could tilt it greater to compensate if wished.   More, over at the same time as building your N.F.T. Systems, try to maintain the channels/gully's as right as feasible. If they sag in spots, water will pool up in one's sones regions. The advocated waft fee anor an N.F.T. Machine is generally among 1/4 gallon to 1/2 of gallon in line with minute (1 to 2 liters) for every develops tube (channel/gully). Or among 15 gallons to 30 gallons in keeping with our (60 to 120 liters). While the plant is simply seedlings, the advocated glide rate may be cut in half of, after which prolonged because the plant life gets larger.

Flow charges a good buy better or lower than those have once in a while been associated with nutrient deficiencies. Also, nutrient deficiencies have now and again been visible when growing tubes (channel/gully) are longer than 30 to 40 toes (10 to 15 meters). However, it's been shown that having a 2nd nutrient feed line 1/2 way down the growing tube (channel/gully) removes that trouble.

Water Culture System

Water's way of life structures is about the best of all six sorts of hydroponic structures. Even as technically easy, they're still very effective for developing plants hydroponically. Now not best do a Water subculture system diagram a lot of domestic hydroponic growers virtually like the usage of water tradition structures, but many business growers use this kind of device on a large scale as well. Specifically, because the water subculture structures is a simple and clean concept. It is also a cheaper sort of device to construct, and another reason why it's famous with home growers as well. Even though the idea is straightforward, there are lots of imaginative approaches to apply and construct water subculture systems out of different substances.

TYPES OF AERATION

Air bubbles

An aquarium air pump and air stones are normally used to offer air bubbles to the nutrient solution for water lifestyle systems, as well as other styles of hydroponic systems. The air pump affords the air extent and is attached to air stones with an airline/tubing. The air stones are made from a porous rock like cloth, and the small pores create small man or woman air bubbles that rise to the pinnacle of the water (nutrient solution).

A soaker hose can be utilized in place of air stones to create the air bubbles as properly. The soaker hose creates even smaller air bubbles. The smaller the air bubbles, the higher for aerating the nutrient answers. Smaller air bubbles offer extra contact floor with the water. The contact among the air bubbles and water allows updating the dissolved oxygen taken up by way of the plant's roots

.

Falling water

Even though now not regular in water subculture structures for domestic growers, floor agitation from falling water splashing around is some other very good manner of aerating the nutrient solution. The higher the water is falling from, and the more quantity of water falling, the extra downward pressure it has while it hits the waters floor.

The more downward pressure, the deeper the agitation and extra aeration (dissolved oxygen) furnished. This technique of aeration is greater, not unusual in business water tradition structures due to the fact they use big volumes of water in comparison to home growers.

Dwc (Deep Water Culture)

The term "DWC" is often used incorrectly when describing water subculture systems. So what is "DWC," and why isn't "DWC" one of the six styles of hydroponic structures? Nicely, it truly is as it's genuinely no longer an exclusive type of hydroponic gadget at all. As you could see by the total name "Deep Water culture," it is just a variation of the already current type of hydroponic gadget called a water tradition device. The phrase "Deep" in the front is best used to describe a few waterways of life systems when the water intensity within the gadget is deeper than 8-10 inches, and then it can be described as an actual DWC machine. However, regardless of the water intensity, DWC structures are still waterways of life systems. Most of the time, the water/nutrient solution depth doesn't want to be deeper than eight inches. That's simply the most effective wish for large plant life, which has large root structures that need extra space and drinks uploads more water. Or while using a container like a bucket that wishes to be filled excessive enough to attain the plant essential root ball near the pinnacle sufficiently. Plants like the size of maximum styles of lettuce can without problems be grown the use of best four-6 inches of water in water culture systems. Now with that stated, their's no distinction between how a standard water culture system and a DWC (deep water tradition) gadget works or capabilities. Their exactly the identical, the handiest difference between the two is the depth of the water inside the device.

Regardless of whether it's an ordinary water culture machine, an actual DWC device, or even a recirculating well-known water lifestyle or proper DWC device, you still want to make certain you've got sufficient water volume and right oxygenation to the root system to support the plants. Even when they reach complete length. Water volume is one of a kind than a water peak. In case you take a gallon of water and pour it in an extensive bucket, the water peak may additionally handiest be an inch or excessive. However, you pour the identical gallon of water in a three-inch wide tube; the water peak may be closer to 2 toes high. So water extent and height are two various things. There may be more about how lots of water extent you ought to be the usage of consistent with plant in this newsletter, "What size reservoir do I need."

The Kratky Method

To begin with, I first need to say the called Kratky approach isn't a brand new or exclusive kind of hydroponic machine. I say, "so-referred to as" because it's, in reality, a simple variation of a standard water tradition gadget, but has sometimes been normally noted with the aid of someone's name (renaming it) alternatively. As a long way as I'm able to inform, the variant turned into dubbed the Kratky technique after B.A. Kratky at the college of Hawaii, who teaches non-recirculating hydroponic methods. On recirculating hydroponic systems (additionally called "run to waste" systems), do not circulate water/nutrient solution from the reservoir to the plant and returned once more to the reservoir. They nevertheless pump water from the reservoir to the plant, however then allow the water/nutrient solution to drain off onto the floor or into a drain gadget to discard any runoff. It sounds wasteful, but non-recirculating systems may be very green and feature little or no runoff if finished properly. Water tradition systems by using definition are non-recirculating, however, can be modified to be circulating structures as nicely.

The hydroponic gadget now and then known as the Kratky approach is a water tradition system without the air pump, as well as element NFT system. It is a water subculture device due to the fact the plant hold above the water/nutrient reservoir the roots grasp down into. It is also part NFT device due to the fact like NFT structures. There is an opening between the basket retaining the plant and water the roots sit in. This gap is an air pocket and is meant to replace the air pump in a preferred water culture system. While the vegetation is small, the basket is supposed to touch the water so the roots can begin growing out the lowest. Because the vegetation develops and the roots get longer, the plant liquids up a number of the water as nicely. That lowers the water level leaving an air hole. Without the air pump to update the dissolved oxygen and oxygenate the water, the plants want the air gap to get the oxygen from. This type of machine layout is useful in places wherein energy is nonexistent or unreliable. But these methods do have its notable drawbacks. The air pump does higher than supply dissolved oxygen in water lifestyle systems. The growing bubbles additionally hold the water is shifting around. While the water/nutrient answer is stagnant, the mineral salts (nutrients) settle close to the lowest. As a result, the nutrient stability will become choppy (very robust near the bottom, and very vulnerable near the top).

The growing air bubbles from the air pump create motion within the water that keeps the nutrient answer mixing all of the time, and as a consequence, nutrients lightly dispensed during the water as well. Also, while the vegetation roots are capable of getting oxygen while the use of the Kratky technique, the roots above the water line cant get nutrients, and the roots underneath the water line cant get oxygen because they have got already depleted the dissolved oxygen within the water early on, and there is nothing to replace it. This is a supply of stress for the plant.

Think of it like being in a swimming pool and no longer being able to move while having your nostrils above water so that you ought to breathe and having your mouth below the water line and able to drink water, so you don't dehydrate. You could survive this manner if you had to. However, it might be very uncomfortable. Plantlife is adaptable and will always attempt to adapt to their surroundings and environment as high-quality they can.

However, the conditions provided while using the Kratky method are some distance from perfect conditions. At the same time as they may be a ways from best conditions, and the value to run an air pump 24/7 and otherwise replace the dissolved oxygen is extraordinarily low. In regions where the energy may be very unreliable or nonexistent, the Kratky technique may be a useful and beneficial choice.

Aeroponic System

While the concept of the aeroponic system is quite easy, it's without a doubt the most technical of all six kinds of hydroponic structures. However, it's still pretty clean to construct your very own primary aeroponic system, and a whole lot of home growers like developing in them as nicely or even get truly suitable outcomes using this type of hydroponic system. Like with every other sort of hydroponic machine, you could use many exceptional varieties of substances to build it, as well as many rare forms of design setups to healthy for your area. Your truly handiest confined with the aid of the space you have got, and your imagination. Some advantages to the use of an aeroponic systems are they generally use little to no developing media. The roots get maximum oxygen, and the plant grows greater unexpectedly as a result. Aeroponic systems also commonly use much less water than other kinds of hydroponic devices (mainly real aeroponic structures). Also, harvesting is usually less complicated, particularly for root crops. However, there are some downsides to aeroponic arrangements as nicely. Except being a chunk greater steeply-priced to construct. The mister/sprinkler heads can clog from the buildup of the dissolved mineral factors within the nutrient answer. So ensure to have extras on hand to swap out when they do clog even as you easy them.

Additionally, because the plant life roots are striking in mid-air through the layout in aeroponic structures, the plant roots are tons extra vulnerable to drying out if there's any interruption within the watering cycle. Therefore, even any transient electricity outage (for any cause) ought to purpose your plant to die a great deal extra quickly than every other form of hydroponic device. Also, there's a discounted margin for mistakes with the nutrient tiers in aeroponic structures, especially the actual high strain systems.

THERE ARE THREE TYPES OF AEROPONIC SYSTEMS

Low-pressure Aeroponic Systems (soakaponics)

Additionally, termed "soakaponics" low strain aeroponic systems are what the majority are familiar with after they think about aeroponics. It's mainly because most all aeroponic systems bought at shops selling hydroponics deliver are low strain structures. While the low strain structures paintings very well, the considerable water droplet length is an awful lot exceptional than inside the excessive strain structures. The main cause the low-pressure aeroponic systems are so famous is they do not require much extra within the manner of fee or particular device than other sorts of hydroponic systems. The simplicity and occasional fee of low strain structures make this type of aeroponic machine very attractive to many domestic growers. Even as you do not need any special equipment or special water pump? The usual fountain/pond pumps will do just pleasant. You do but want a pump; it truly is more potent than you will for another sort of hydroponic gadget. This is the principle and most essential difference. It is because the strain inside the machine will drop a few with each sprinkler head you add. Fountain and pond pumps don't give a psi (pressure) rating, but the extra GPH (gallons in keeping with our) it may place out closer to the "max head height" the stronger (extra pressure) the pump has. You may want sufficient sprinkler heads that the spray overlaps, and completely covers the entire root area. While the plant gets bigger and the foundation mass receives bigger. As the basis mass receives big, it's regularly hard for the spray from the sprinkler heads to penetrate the thick root mass. In case you design your low strain aeroponic gadget, so the roots are sprayed from above the basis mass or near the top of it, the water will trickle down through the foundation mass a whole lot better than trying to spray them from underneath.

High-pressure Aeroponic Systems (accurate aeroponic systems)

While the low-pressure structures are the most common, excessive stress aeroponic systems are the "true aeroponic" systems. This is as it takes the higher strain (60-90 psi) to properly atomize the water into a gentle mist with a tiny water droplet size. This fine mist lets in the roots to get loads greater oxygen than in low-stress structures. However, it's more complex and steeply-priced to build an excessive strain aeroponic machine.

Ultrasonic foggers

Ultrasonic foggers have additionally been used to create a mist in aeroponic structures, but with combined results. Ultrasonic foggers are maximum usually used to create visible displays in ponds, in addition to on degree. They're also often offered around Halloween with the Halloween decorations too. While they do create a mist with a totally small water droplet length, there's very little real moisture within the mist/fog.The mist constituted of ultrasonic foggers additionally tends to drop to the lowest of the box. Making it difficult to ensure the roots are entirely protected using the mist all of the time. Any other trouble with the use of foggers is that the plates tend to clog with mineral increase. The most effective plates which have shown to work with any reliability are the extra high-priced Teflon heads. They can now and then be wiped clean the usage of white vinegar, or water and pH down, and wiping them off with a Q-tip. A few growers have mixed the use of ultrasonic foggers at the side of the low-pressure aeroponic design in the equal gadget.

Chapter 5

Best Plants And Beneficial Insects
For Hydroponic Systems

HIGH-QUALITY PLANT FOR HYDROPONIC SYSTEMS

The five first-class plant life to develop in a hydroponic device are:

- Lettuce

- Spinach

- Strawberries

- Bell Peppers

- Herbs

Growers have observed that those florae take to hydroponics like a duck to water. They're durable, fast-growing, and don't carry quite a few works to get commenced – all essential functions that supply a brand new grower a little wiggle room!

Now allow's observe every of these a bit closer:

Lettuce In Hydroponics

Lettuce (and most other leafy vegetables) must be your first plant to strive with a hydroponic machine. These plants have a shallow root system that matches their brief above-ground height. Which means there's no need to tie stakes or set publications for the plant. As a substitute, you allow them to develop while frequently converting their nutrient solution. In the end, they'll appearance exact enough to consume, and you could!

- **Grow time:** about 30 days

- **best pH:** 6.Zero to 7.Zero

- **Tip:** Stagger plantings, so you have a continuous delivery of lunchtime lettuce!

- **range options:** Romaine, Boston, Iceberg, Buttercrunch, Bibb

Spinach In Hydroponics

Spinach grows quickly in a hydroponic device, mainly when using the Nutrient movie approach or other techniques that keep the nutrient solution incredibly oxygenated. You'll also use a long way much less water than an in-the-ground lawn. It's clean to begin that flora from seed, and per week after sprouting, move them into your machine.

- **Develop time:** about forty days

- **first-class pH:** 6.Zero to 7.Five

- **Tip:** For sweeter spinach, preserve your develop temperatures between sixty-five levels F and seventy two levels F. The lower temperatures may additionally slow grow time, even though.

- **range options:** Savoy, Bloomsdale, clean Leafed, Regiment, Catalina, Tyee, purple Cardinal

Strawberries In Hydroponics

The worst thing approximately fruits is how seasonal they're. In case you don't get them domestically while the crop is prepared, you're counting on trucked-in berries that start deteriorating as soon as they're picked. With hydroponics, you could have a ready-to-devour crop of strawberries all 12 months long. Harvesting is superb-handy as correctly – no bending over! Fruits seem to do first-class with an ebb and glide machine, but deep water culture or nutrient movie approach can do for a small crop.

- **Develop time:** approximately 60 days

- **Best pH:** five.5 to six.2

- **Tip:** Don't purchase strawberry seeds, which won't be berry-prepared for years. As a substitute, you want to buy cold-stored runners, which might be already at that level.

- **Variety alternatives:** Brighton, Chandler, Douglass, red Gauntlet, Tioga

Bell Peppers In Hydroponics

Bell peppers are a barely new advanced hydroponic plant. Don't allow them to develop to their full height, as an alternative, prune and pinch plant life at about 8 inches to spur pepper increase. Deep water way of life or ebb and float systems are first-rate for peppers.

- Grow time: about ninety days

- excellent pH: 6.0 to six. Five

- **Tip:** Plan to offer up to 18 hours of mild for that vegetation every day, and lift your mild rack as the vegetation develop, retaining flora approximately 6 inches from the lights.

- **variety options:** Ace, California wonder, Vidi, Yolo surprise

Herbs In Hydroponics

There is a wide form of herbs that paintings splendidly in hydroponic gardening. Studies have proven that hydroponic herbs are more flavorful and aromatic than those grown within the area. What herb do you want to grow? Basil, chives, cilantro, dill, mint, oregano, parsley, rosemary, thyme, and watercress are all brilliant options. Herb manufacturing is another excellent way to check out your new hydroponic system, and nearly every gadget fashion is appropriate for a spherical of herbs as you study the ropes!

- **develop time:** Varies by plant

- **first-rate pH:** Varies via plant

- **Tip:** Flush your growing medium about as soon as every week to do away with any greater vitamins that your flora hasn't (or received) soak up.

Beneficial Insects

Not all bugs are horrific pests. There are a few insect species called helpful bugs that may provide a long-term sustainable pest manipulate solution through preying on the bugs that do a splendid deal of harm for your garden and outdoor plant.

Useful insects are taken into consideration an organic manage solution, which refers to methods of controlling pests the use of different living organisms. Here's a listing of beneficial insects to bear in mind:

Useful insects for Pest control

In no precise order, right here are fourteen beneficial insects to recall for natural pest manipulate. You may learn about what they prey on, what habitat they are acceptable for, vegetation that attracts the beneficial insects, and traditional fees.

1. Ladybug

- **Preys:** aphids, whitefly, mites, fleas, Colorado potato beetle

- **Attracted by:** Dill, Dandelion, Fern-leaf Yellow, Basket of Gold, commonplace Yarrow

- **Information:** Ladybugs can eat other than 5,000

aphids at some point in their lifetime.

2. Praying Mantis

- **Preys:** extensive range including caterpillars, moths, beetles, and crickets

- **Attracted by using:** tall grasses and shrubs, cosmos, marigolds, dills

- **Statistics:** Mantis can flip their heads 180 stages to view their surroundings.

2. Spiders

- **Preys:** wide range which includes mattress bugs, aphids, roaches, grasshoppers, mosquitoes, and fruit flies

- **Attracted via:** tall plant life for weaving spiders, mulch for predatory spiders

- **Information:** maximum spiders whole their existence cycle in one year.

3. Flour Beetles

- **Preys:** slugs, caterpillars, ants, Colorado potato beetles, cutworms

- **Attracted by:** evening primrose, amaranthus, clover

- **Data:** floor beetles are generally handiest energetic at night time.

4. Aphid Midges

- **Preys:** aphids

- **Attracted using** Dills, vegetation with lots of pollen and nectar, the supply of water

- **Facts:** aphid midges can assault over sixty types of aphid species.

5. Braconid Wasps

- **Preys:** tobacco hornworm, tomato hornworm, caterpillars, aphids

- **Attracted through:** Fern-leaf Yarrow, commonplace Yarrow, Dill, Lemon Balm, Parsley

- **Information:** Braconid wasps kill hornworms through laying eggs within the caterpillar.

6. Damsel bugs

- **Preys:** caterpillars, mites, aphids, potato beetles, cabbage worms

- **Attracted by:** Caraway, Fennel, Alfalfa, Spearmint, Peter Pan Goldenrod

- **Information:** damsel worm populations can thrive in case you offer them opportunity locations to hide.

7. Inexperienced Lacewings

- **Preys:** aphids, whitefly, leafhopper, mealybugs, caterpillars of pest moths

- **Attracted through:** Dill, Angelica, Golden Marguerite, Coriander, Dandelion

- **Information:** the larvae do the actual process of having rid of smooth-bodied pests.

8. Minute Pirate insects

- **Preys:** spider mites, insect eggs, caterpillars, aphids, thrips

- **Attracted using** Caraway, Fennel, Alfalfa, Spearmint, Peter Pan Goldenrod

- **Data:** both immature stages and adults prey on an expansion of small insects.

9. Soldier Beetles

- **Preys:** grasshopper eggs, aphids, gentle-bodied bugs

- **Attracted by way of** goldenrod, zinnia, marigold, linden timber

- **Records:** soldier beetles do now not harm plants and are harmless to people.

10.   Tachinid Flies

- **Preys:** gypsy moths, jap beetles, cutworms, squash bugs

- **Attracted by way of** carrots, cilantro, dill, coriander, buckwheat

- **Statistics:** Tachinids parasitize pests by using laying eggs onto the host or onto nearby foliage.

11.   Hoverflies

- **Preys:** aphids, scale insects, caterpillars

- **Attracted by way of** Fern-leaf Yarrow, commonplace Yarrow, Dill, Basket of Gold, Statice

- **Statistics:** Hoverfly larvae feed on pests, while the adult flies feed on pollen.

12.   Mealybug Destroyer

- **Preys:** mealybugs (now not all species)

- **Attracted with the aid of** fennel, dill, angelica, sunflower, goldenrod

- **Information:** One mealybug destroyer can devour up to 250 mealybug larvae.

13.   Predatory Mites

- **Preys:** spider mites

- **Attracted by way of** humid environments like greenhouses and excessive tunnels

- **Facts:** predatory mites feed at the pollen, and now not the plant itself when prey is unavailable.

Chapter 6

Most Occurring Problems And How To Fix Them

Hydroponics is an impressive manner to grow the plant at domestic this is hard, a laugh, and worthwhile. However, there are some of the troubles with hydroponics that you could come across, and it's miles critical to discover ways to keep away from those or cope with them efficiently.

Hydroponic growing is a more significant technical talent than developing flora in the soil. You could analyze plenty from analyzing books and articles and watching academic motion pictures. But, one of the friendly approaches to study is from our errors. Fortunately, I've made lots of mistakes even as growing plants with hydroponics over the years.

1. HYDROPONICS DEVICE LEAKS

Device leaks can occur for a whole sort of motive. Leaks can arise at any joins or valves to your gadget. They can also occur if your system receives blocked, including while the foundation mass clogs up an NFT machine, main to water backing up and overflowing. Leaks can also happen if you build a device with a reservoir which can't keep all the nutrient solution inside the device. In this situation, an electricity cut or pump failure may also lead to a return up to an overflow of your reservoir.

Solution

Test your device previous to planting anything. Tighten any valves and make sure all connections are tight and at ease. Regularly test your device for troubles such as root overgrowth or clogged drains or stores. Ensure that you choose a reservoir that can quite keep all the nutrient solution within the machine, now not just the quantity that is in it while the gadget is in use. In case you are using an indoor device, take into account placing it on a water-resistant surface or, if viable, on a drip tray in case you are using a small device. This is an excellent idea to seize leaks but may also reduce mess while tending on your device.

2. BUYING CHEAP, INADEQUATE OR WRONG LIGHTS

I like to use my hydroponics systems indoors so that I will develop sparkling greens all 12 months-round. Without sufficient lighting fixtures of the correct kind, the performance of a machine may be very disappointing. I've made various errors with indoor development lighting fixtures, which include shopping for cheap lighting that has been inadequate for what I wished or buying the incorrect sort of lights that caused terrible fruit and vegetable yields.

Solution

For most of the people, I might strongly endorse searching at LED, and T5 fluorescent develops lights. Those are usually the easiest to apply and can be suitable for most users. In case you are shopping for LED develop lights, do not go for the most inexpensive alternative. Do a chunk of research and purchase high-quality lighting on the way to produce light at the appropriate wavelengths and insufficient portions in your gadget. Make sure you are buying sufficient develop lighting fixtures on your device. An excellent rule of thumb is to calculate the square footage of the cover of your grow area and multiply this through 65.

3. THE USAGE OF THE INCORRECT FERTILIZER

While growing plants in soil, some of the micronutrients wanted are already gift within the soil in enough portions. For this reason, fertilizer designed for developing plant life in the soil does not wish to to encompass most of the hint micro vitamins, which might be critical for healthy plant boom.

Solution

Ensure you buy vitamins designed to be used with hydroponics. You may make your hydroponics fertilizer from scratch. However, it is an awful lot simpler to shop for a two or 3 component answer. This will be blended to supply nutrient solution that can be adjusted to maximum plant and boom phases.

4. NOT KEEPING MATTERS SMOOTH

If you allow your hydroponics setup and the area around it come to be messy and grimy, you could grow the chance of spreading sickness or pests for your hydroponic system. A part of the cleansing procedure is to forestall algae, illnesses, and parasites from being capable of establishing themselves to your system. Even as a few humans do run systems specially designed to inspire the boom of beneficial microorganisms, I suppose for most home hydroponics setups, it is higher to avoid the pathogenic organisms, via frequently cleansing your machine and surrounding location.

Solution

Hold the vicinity around your hydroponics setup clean and properly prepared. Every 2-three weeks, drain the device, flush the growing media and roots with water and smooth the reservoir, pumps, and tubing.

5. NOT GETTING TO KNOW AS YOU CROSS

Each crop of vegetation in a hydroponics system is specific. Some things will pass well, and you will come across a few issues, both minor and foremost. You must take the opportunity to analyze what went nicely and what went incorrect, to adjust your exercise for future plants.

Solution

Record, picture, and take note of the most cooling and awful elements of every gadget you use and crop you grow. While you stumble upon a hassle, search for a solution. Books, web sites, and Youtube have so many statistics to be had that you may be able to resolve your issues or save you them the subsequent time.

6. NOT TRACKING THE HEALTH OF YOUR PLANT LIFE

If you do not display your plant regularly, you will miss the early signs and symptoms of troubles. Whether this is an insufficient boom or signs of deficiency or disorder, the sooner you realize there may be a problem, the extra risk you have got of correcting it and now not ruining your plant life.

Solution

Display the boom and circumstance of your vegetation regularly. While you see a hassle, make an effort to discover what the trouble is, and try to correct it. In case you word sickness or pests, treat early, and you may be able to prevent immoderate harm to your flora.

7. NOT MONITORING AND ADJUSTING THE PH STAGE

The pH degree of your nutrient answer is one of the maximum essential elements of hydroponic development. While developing flora in soil, the soil itself acts as a pH buffer and prevents fast adjustments inside the pH degree. Because of this, pH troubles are slower to increase and can be dealt with more without problems. This isn't the case for hydroponics. The pH can trade appreciably over hours or days because of a range of things such as temperature, charge of absorption of vitamins by your vegetation, presence of sickness, excess evaporation, and so on.

Solution

When growing with hydroponics, you must display the pH of your nutrient answer. In a new device or while current changes have been made, you may want to check and regulate the pH on each day's foundation. In a reliable tool, you can reduce trying out a couple of times in keeping with the week. As you gain experience with hydroponic growing, you may begin to understand the elements that could influence the pH, and you may get a feel for how frequently to check. The excellent alternatives for checking out pH are to apply a pH testing kit or a pH testing meter. I usually propose getting a first-rate satisfactory electric pH checking out the meter because it makes pH testing brief and straightforward.

8. NUTRIENT DEFICIENCY AND TOXICITY

Numerous elements could reason nutrient deficiency or toxicity to your plant life. It's no longer consistently clean to tell which nutrient is inflicting the problem or whether deficiency or toxicity is the trouble. There are various signs to appearance out for to detect deficiency and toxicity of numerous vitamins, and you'll get higher at identifying issues with time and experience.PH, temperature, plant increase rate, nutrient answer concentration, consumer mistakes, and a whole host of other factors can purpose nutrient problems. Don't forget that excess levels of 1 nutrient can reason trouble with the absorption of every other.

Solution

Make sure to make up your nutrient solution cautiously and appropriately. Make sure that the water you're using to make up your nutrient answer isn't excessively troublesome. If so, remember diluting it with distilled water or using water that has been through a reverse osmosis filter or activated carbon filter out to reduce the extent of dissolved solids.

Monitor and regulate the pH of your nutrient answer. In case your plant starts to display symptoms of nutrient deficiency or toxicity, my advice is to flush your device, discard the nutrient answer, and make up a sparkling batch. More skilled growers might also have the talents to alter matters as they move; however, maximum novices and intermediates will be higher to take the safe method.

11. BLOCKED OR BROKEN PUMPS AND SPRAY NOZZLES

Hydroponics systems rely on regular or widespread shipping of water and nutrients to your plant. When you have a pump or nozzle failure or blockage, those can result in troubles very quickly. A broken or blocked water pump can cause plants in maximum structures being cut off from their water supply. Wick and DWC systems will no longer have this problem. For aeroponic structures, it's far pretty not unusual for the spray nozzles to get clogged over time. If this occurs, the exposed roots will dry out very swiftly, main to your plants wilting and loss of life very quickly. Air pumps also can fail. It doesn't take long for the vegetation to cause the tiers of dissolved oxygen within the water to drop to the degree that the roots begin to drown, which can bring about the loss of life.

Solution

Test your gadget often. Consider buying water or air pump with a built-in alarm, so that it will sound if there is a blockage. Don't forget designing your gadget, so that if there's a blockage or failure, it's going to now not result in rapid plant demise. For NFT technique structures as an example, a great choice is to go away the water outlet slightly raised on the stop of the channel, so that it will result in a small pool of water, to remain inside the event of a pump failure.

12. DECIDING ON THE INCORRECT GROWING MEDIUM

The selection of growing media is enormous, and there are many factors to don't forget while creating a choice. I've some other complete article handling choosing the right growing medium in case you want to study extra. Some developing media are reusable, and a few are virtually the most uncomplicated suitable to be used once. A few are absorbent and will keep water across the plant roots. Some are minimally absorbent and permit fast drainage. A few are luxurious, and some are cheap. Many growing media can be adapted to paintings in exceptional hydroponics structures, and one-of-a-kind growers could have their preferences.

Solution

- Take a chunk of time to reflect on consideration on what you need your growing media to do.

- Study around to analyze what other human beings have had maximum success with.

- Recall your price range and whether or not you need to reuse the media for multiple developing cycles.

- Examine my article about growing media, and also you received cross too a long way wrong.

14. CONSTRUCTING AN INCONVENIENT HYDROPONICS SYSTEM

Numerous things can grow the inconvenience of a hydroponics device. Setting a system in a small space without ok room to work around it or placing it someplace that your equipment isn't close to hand can get frustrating. A machine that doesn't have a handy water supply will cause you remorse down the road. A poorly built DIY machine that is vulnerable to leaks or failure will handiest cause you frustration.

Solution

Begin small. Whether or not it's far a DIY gadget or a pre-constructed system, your first few growing cycles ought to be considered as a getting to know enjoy. In case you make horrific choices at the outset, you can pass on and plan something better next time. Plan your hydroponics machine – You need to have your system and water supply near hand and somewhere next to the system that you can put together nutrient answer or smooth your gadget. If you are growing inside, reflect on consideration on what would possibly happen if there may be a leak. Is your floor water-resistant, or may want to you positioned down a drip tray.

15. PLANT ILLNESSES

Hydroponic vegetation is commonly much less liable to sickness than plant life grown in soil. Without soil, microorganisms and fungi have less opportunity to establish themselves. Nevertheless, favorable conditions, inclusive of extra humidity, high temperatures, and lack of direct daylight, can significantly boom the risk of your vegetation growing sicknesses, which could threaten your entire crop. Diverse functions of your system also can motive extra pressure on your plants that can lead them to greater prone to disease.

Solution

To save your sickness on your hydroponic plant, you have to try and avoid situations that pathogens will thrive in. This means keeping off excessively excessive temperatures and humidity levels and trying to make sure that your flora receives some direct sunlight or accurate great synthetic light. Monitor the pH and attention of your nutrient answer. Make sure that your nutrient answer incorporates all of the vital macro and micronutrients that your vegetation requires to increase. Screen your plant often for any symptoms of the ailment. If you be aware of a problem, attempt to perceive the cause and deal with it as quickly as viable.

ENVIRONMENTAL FACTORS AFFECTING PLANT GROWTH

Plant growth and geographic distribution are many sufferings from the surroundings. If any environmental component is much less than best, it limits a plant's boom and distribution. For instance, the simplest flora tailored to limited quantities of water can live in deserts. Either without delay or indirectly, maximum plant troubles are caused by environmental strain. In a few instances, unfortunate ecological situations (e.g., too little water) harm a plant immediately. In other cases, environmental stress weakens a plant and makes it more vulnerable to disease or insect attack. Environmental factors that affect plant increase include mild, temperature, water, humidity, and vitamins.

It's far vital to apprehend how these factors affect plant boom and development. With primary know-how of these elements, you may be able to manipulate flora to fulfill your needs, whether or not for elevated leaf, flower, or fruit production. Using spotting the jobs of these factors, you also will be better capable of diagnosing plant problems resulting from environmental stress.

LIGHT

Three principal characteristics of light affect plant growth: quantity, quality, and duration.

Quantity

Light quantity refers back to the depth or concentration of sunlight. It varies with the seasons. The most amount of light is found in the summertime and the minimal in winter. Up to a degree, the extra sunlight a plant receives, the more its ability to generate meals via photosynthesis. You could manage light amounts to acquire unusual plant boom patterns.

Increase mild via surrounding plant with reflective substances, a white historical past, or supplemental lights. Decrease it with the aid of shading vegetation with cheesecloth or woven color cloths.

Quality

Mild satisfactory refers back to the shade (wavelength) of mild. Daylight materials the whole range of wavelengths and may be broken up by way of a prism into bands of red, orange, yellow, inexperienced, blue, indigo, and violet. Blue and pink light, which plant soak up, have the finest effect on plant increase. Blue mild is accountable usually for vegetative (leaf) growth. Red light, while mixed with blue mild, encourages flowering. Flora appearance green to us due to the fact they replicate, as opposed to taking in, inexperienced mild. Knowing which light source to apply is vital for manipulating plant boom. For example, fluorescent (cool white) light is high inside the blue wavelength. It encourages leafy growth and is fantastic for beginning seedlings.

Incandescent light is excessive in the red or orange variety but produces typically too much heat to be a precious light source for plant life. Fluorescent develop-lighting tries to imitate sunlight with a mixture of red and blue wavelengths. However, they are high priced and usually no better than ordinary fluorescent lighting fixtures.

Duration

Length, or photoperiod, refers to the quantity of time a plant is uncovered to mild. Photoperiod controls flowering in many plants (determine 26). Scientists to begin with concept the duration of light length triggered flowering and different responses inside vegetation. Accordingly, they describe plants as short-day or long-day, relying on what conditions they flower underneath.

We now realize that it isn't the period of the light period, but as a substitute, the length of uninterrupted darkness, that is essential to plant improvement. Vegetation is classified into three categories: quick-day (lengthy-night), long-day (quick-night time), or day-neutral, relying on their reaction to the length of light or darkness. Quick-day plant shape plant simplest while day duration is less than about 12 hours. Much spring- and fall-flowering vegetation, along with chrysanthemum, poinsettia, and yuletide cactus, are on this category.

In assessment, lengthy-day plant form plants most effective while day duration exceeds 12 hours. Maximum summer flowering flora (e.g., rudbeckia, California poppy, and aster), in addition to many veggies (beet, radish, lettuce, spinach, and potato), are in this category.

Temperature

Temperature impacts most plant processes, including photosynthesis, transpiration, respiration, germination, and flowering. As temperature increases (up to a degree), photosynthesis, transpiration, and respiration increase. While combined with day-duration, temperature also influences the trade from vegetative (leafy) to reproductive (flowering) boom. Depending on the situation and the specific plant, the impact of temperature can either speed up or sluggish down this transition.

Photosynthesis And Respiration

Thermoperiod refers to everyday temperature alternate. Plants develop first-class while daylight hour's temperature is set 10 to fifteen stages higher than the middle of the night temperature. Under these situations, plant life photosynthesizes (increase) and respire (destroy down) at some stage in ultimate daylight temperatures, after which curtail breathing at night time. But, now, not all floras develop first-rate beneath the identical range among nighttime and daylight hour's temperatures. For example, snapdragons grow pleasant at the hours of darkness temperatures of fifty 5°F; poinsettias, at sixty 2°F.Temperatures higher than wished increase respiration, once in a while above the rate of photosynthesis. Therefore, photosynthetic are used faster than they are produced. For growth to occur, photosynthesis has to be extra than respiration. Daylight hour's temperatures, which can be too low, frequently produce terrible increases by way of slowing down photosynthesis. The result is decreased yield (i.e., fruit or grain manufacturing).).

Water And Humidity

Maximum developing vegetation incorporates approximately 90 percent of water. Water plays many jobs in plant life. Its miles:

- A primary component in photosynthesis and respiration

- Responsible for turgor pressure in cells (Like the air in an inflated balloon, water is accountable for the fullness and firmness of plant tissue. Turgor is wanted to preserve free form and make certain mobile growth.)

- A solvent for minerals and carbohydrates moving via the plant

- Liable for cooling leaves because it evaporates from leaf tissue for the duration of transpiration

- A regulator of stomatal starting and remaining, for this reason controlling transpiration and, to some degree, photosynthesis

- The source of pressure to transport roots through the soil

The medium in which most biochemical reactions take vicinity

The relative humidity is the ratio of water vapor inside the air to the amount of water the air could hold at the modern-day temperature and pressure. Heat air can preserve greater water vapor than cold air. Relative humidity (RH) is expressed via the following equation:

- RH = water in air ÷ water air could preserve (at regular temperature and pressure)

The relative humidity is given as a percent. As an example, if a pound of air at 75°F should maintain four grams of water vapor, and there are most effective 3 grams of water in the air, then the relative humidity (RH) is:

- 3 ÷ 4 = zero.Seventy five = seventy five%

Water vapor moves from a place of high relative humidity to one of low relative humidity. The extra the distinction in humidity, the quicker water moves. This thing is crucial because the charge of water motion immediately influences a plant's transpiration rate. The relative humidity within the air spaces among leaf cells processes 100 percent.

While a stoma opens, water vapor within the leaf rushes out into the encircling air (figure 25), and a bubble of excessive humidity bureaucracy around the stoma. Through saturating this small region of air, the bubble reduces the difference in relative humidity between the air spaces inside the leaf and the air adjoining to the leaf. As a result, transpiration slows down. If the wind blows the humidity bubble away, but, transpiration increases.

Consequently, transpiration typically is at its peak on warm, dry, windy days. On the other hand, transpiration generally is pretty sluggish while temperatures are cold, humidity is high, and there's no wind. Warm, dry situations usually arise at some point in the summer season, which in part explains why flora wilt fast within the summer. If a regular supply of water isn't always to be had to be absorbed through the roots and moved to the leaves, turgor pressure is lost, and leaves move limp.

Plant Nutrition

Plant nutrition often is confused with fertilization. Plant nutrients refer to a plant's need for and use of simple chemical elements. Fertilization is the term used when these substances are brought to the surroundings around a plant. Loads ought to take place earlier than a chemical element in fertilizer may be utilized by a plant. Flora wants 17 factors for ordinary boom. Three of them--carbon, hydrogen, and oxygen--are located in air and water. The relaxation is determined within the soil. Six soil elements are known as macronutrients because they are used in exceedingly massive quantities through the plant. They may be nitrogen, potassium, magnesium, calcium, phosphorus, and sulfur.

Fertilizers

Fertilizers are substances containing plant vitamins which are introduced to the environment around a plant. Usually, they're delivered to the water or soil; however, some may be sprayed on leaves. This technique is referred to as foliar fertilization. It must be accomplished carefully with a dilute solution; due to the fact, and close fertilizer attention can injure leaf cells. The nutrient, but does want to skip through the thin layer of wax (cutin) at the leaf surface. Fertilizers are not plant food! Vegetation produces its very own food from water, carbon dioxide, and solar strength through photosynthesis. This food (sugars and carbohydrates) is combined with plant vitamins to supply proteins, enzymes, vitamins, and different factors crucial to increase.

Nutrient Absorption

Whatever that reduces or stops sugar production in leaves can lower nutrient absorption. Consequently, if a plant is underneath pressure due to low mild or intense temperatures, nutrient deficiency may develop. A plant's developmental degree or price of boom also may additionally affect the number of nutrients absorbed. Many plants have a relaxation (dormant) length throughout the part of the yr. At some point in this time, few nutrients are absorbed. Plantlife also may additionally take in specific vitamins as flower buds begin to develop than they do during intervals of fast vegetative growth.

Chapter 7

Understanding the Types Of Rock

A number of the most extensively used developing media's include Rockwool, lightweight increased Clay aggregate (called, Hydrocorn or develop Rock), Coconut Fiber/Coconut chips, and Perlite or Vermiculite. At the same time, as several substances may be used as growing media in hydroponics, they could all have very exceptional assets than every other form of media. We have even seen the usage of hay bales as a growing medium to develop tomatoes, using drip strains on top to drip the nutrient answer onto the hay bales and tomato plant roots. There isn't always one growing media; this is higher than the relaxation. Mainly with so many ones of a kind, hydroponic system designs possible. However, many growers, in the end, prefer one type over others. There are lots of factors to remember when choosing what to apply as a developing media. The sort of machine you're developing in and the way you design and construct that device is the most massive aspect. Even as there is no one first-rate developing media for all situations, a few developing media's paintings higher than others in individual structures. With any hydroponic device and any growing media, the aim continues to be identical. You want the roots to be wet, no longer soggy and saturated. If the growing media is soaked and mushy, the roots will suffocate from the loss of oxygen. That situation can effortlessly lead to roots dying, and root rot.

ROCKWOOL

Rockwool is one of the maximum commonplace growing media used in hydroponics. Rockwool is a sterile, porous, nondegradable medium that is composed in most cases of granite and limestone that is terrifically heated and melted, then spun into a small threads like cotton candy. The Rockwool is then formed into blocks, sheets, cubes, slabs, or flocking. Rockwool sucks up water without difficulty, so you'll want to be cautious no longer to allow it turn out to be saturated, or it can suffocate your plant roots, as well as cause stem rot and root rot. Rockwool has to be pH balanced before use. It's accomplished by soaking it in pH balanced water earlier than use.

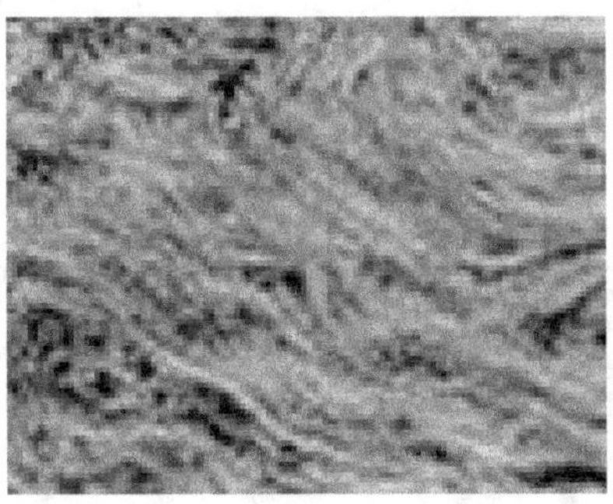

DEVELOP ROCK (HYDROCORN)

Hydrocorn develops rockGrow rock is a light-weight increased Clay combination (L.E.C.A.), which may be a form of clay that's brilliant-fired to create a porous texture. It is heavy enough to provide comfortable help for your plants, however, nevertheless mild weight. Grow rocks are a non-degradable, sterile developing medium that holds moisture, has a neutral pH, and will also wick up nutrient technique to the root structures of your plant. Hydrocorn develop media is reusable; it can be wiped clean, sterilized, then reused again. Even though on a massive scale, cleaning and sterilizing huge quantities of developing rocks may be quite time eating. Develop rock is one of the most famous developing mediums used for hydroponics, and just about everyone keeps promoting hydroponics supplies includes it.

COCO FIBER   COCO CHIPS

"Coco coir" (Coconut fiber) is from the outer husk of coconuts. What becomes once considered a waste product, is one of the high-quality developing mediums to be had. Although coco coir is natural plant material, it breaks down and decomposes very slowly, so it might not provide any nutrients to the flora growing in it, making it perfect for hydroponics. Coco coir is likewise pH impartial, holds moisture thoroughly, but still allows for proper aeration for the roots. Coco fiber comes in two paperwork, coco coir (fiber), and coco chips.

They are each fabricated from coconut husks, and the most useful distinction is the particle length. The coco fiber particle length is about the same as potting soil, while the coco chips particle length is more like small wooden chips. The bigger size of the coco chips permits for larger air pockets between particles, consequently allowing even higher aeration for the roots. Additionally, in case your using baskets to develop your plant in, the chips are too large to fall through the slats in the hampers.

Each the fiber and chips come in compressed bricks, and once soaked in water, it expands to approximately six times the different length. Coco fiber does tend to color the water, but that diminishes over the years. And you may reach out most of the shade in case you soak it in warm/warm water sometimes earlier than use.

PERLITE

Perlite hydroponic developing mediumPerlite is mainly composed of minerals that are subjected to very excessive heat, which then extend it like popcorn, so it turns into very lightweight, porous, and absorbent. Perlite has an impartial pH, notable wicking movement, and is very porous. Perlite can via used by itself or blended with other styles of developing media. However, because perlite is so mild that it floats, relying on the way you designed your hydroponic machine, perlite using itself might not be the pleasant preference of developing media for flood and drain structures.

Perlite is extensively utilized in potting soils, and any nursery needs to deliver baggage of it. However, perlite is once in a while extensively utilized as an additive introduced to cement. You could locate it for a higher price with the constructing deliver's, and at locations that sell concrete mixes and combining deliver's. When operating with perlite, be careful no longer to get any of the dust to your eyes. Rinse it off to scrub out the dust, and wet it down before running with it to keep the dust from going airborne.

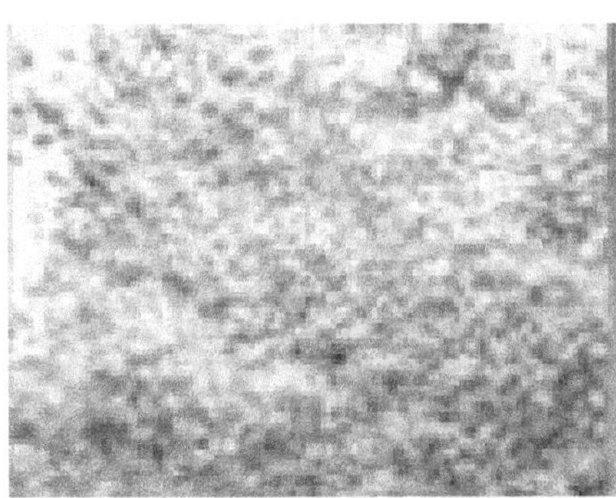

VERMICULITE

Developing mediumVermiculite is a silicate mineral that, like perlite, expands while uncovered to very high warmness. As a growing media, vermiculite is pretty just like perlite besides that it has a pretty excessive cation-alternate capacity, meaning it can preserve vitamins for later use. Additionally, just like the perlite, vermiculite is very light and tends to go with the flow. There are different makes use of and kinds of vermiculite so that you'll want to make certain what you get is intended for horticulture use. The very best manner to be sure is to get it from a nursery.

OASIS CUBES

Oasis cubesOasis Cubes are just like Rockwool cubes and have similar belongings. But oasis cubes are extra just like the inflexible inexperienced or white floral foam utilized by forests to preserve the stems in their floral arrangements. Oasis cubes are an open mobile cloth, which means that the cells can soak up water and air. The open cells wick moisture at some point of the fabric, and the roots can without problems grow and increase via the open mobile structure. At the same time, as oasis cubes are commonly used as starter cubes for hydroponically grown plants, they also have bags you could fill your developing boxes with. Even as oasis cubes are much like Rockwool, Oasis cubes do not come to be waterlogged as without problems as Rockwool cubes. Nevertheless, do not allow it to live in consistent contact with the water supply, or you'll still have water logging issues.

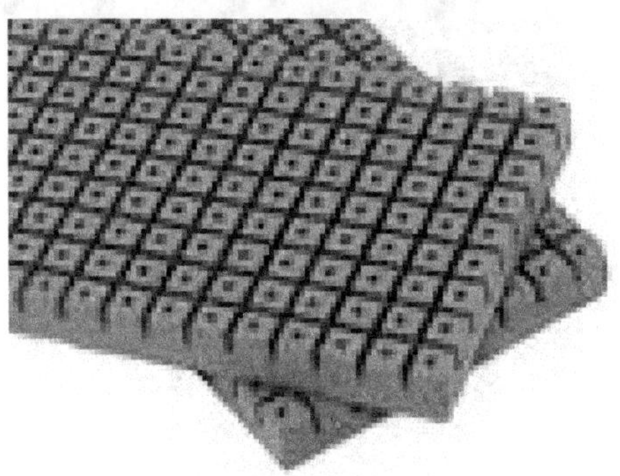

FLORAL FOAM

Floral foam can be used as a growing media in hydroponics as properly, and is just like the oasis cubes, though the cellular size is greater within the floral foam. Depending on the sort of hydroponic device your the usage of, and how you designed it, you may observe more than one problem with using floral foam. First, it can collapse easily, and that may leave particles for your water. 2d you may need to make sure it does not get waterlogged. The floral foam absorbs water without difficulty, so make sure it is not inconsistent in touch with the water delivery.

GROWSTONE HYDROPONIC SUBSTRATE

GrowstonesGrowstones are crafted from recycled glass. They're like grow rocks (hydro corn) but are made of clay and shaped marbles. Growstones are lightweight, erratically fashioned, porous, and reusable. They provide desirable aeration and moisture to the root sector. They have exact wicking potential and might wick water up to 4 inches above the waterline. So that you'll need to make certain, it has suitable drainage or is deep sufficient, so it doesn't wick water to the top. Otherwise, like with the growing media in any hydroponic device, if the pinnacle of the developing media is usually wet, you may have trouble with stem rot. While they're crafted from recycled glass, their now not sharp, and you won't get reduce from it, although they ruin.

RIVER ROCK

River rock is not unusual and easy to find in domestic improvement shops, in addition to even puppy delivery shops (with the fish and aquariums). River rock in all fairness inexpensive (depending on wherein you get it from), and is derived in many specific sizes. River rock is rounded with smooth edges from tumbling down the river. Although manufactured river rock is rounded the use of large mechanical tumblers, it has the same give up end result with easy edges. You can use everyday rocks out of your again yard in hydroponic structures as well in case you don't mind the jagged edges. Simply ensure to smooth and sanitize them before the usage of it. Just spray all the dirt off of the rock the use of the jet spray out of your hose to smooth it, then soak it overnight in bleach water to sanitize it. Then rinse and use. Though the usage of rock as a developing media is less expensive and easy, it will get heavy fast, so that you won't need to move it later. River rocks aren't porous. Therefore it does not maintain and preserve moisture inside the root zone of hydroponic systems. Rock is choppy, so it has a whole lot of air pockets between the rocks so the roots can get plenty of oxygen, but water effortlessly drains down to the lowest. Rock may not wick up moisture either, so you will want to modify your watering schedules, so the roots do not dry out among watering's. You may blend in a few coco chips or different developing media that hold moisture together with your rock to useful resource it in keeping onto moisture longer.

Because of the best drainage belongings of rock, it is excellent to apply to useful resources in the drainage of different hydroponic developing media that might otherwise come to be saturated from sitting in water. A layer of rock at the bottom of the growing field will preserve your developing media from sitting in water at the bottom of the box, maintaining it from being saturated.

PINE SHAVINGS

Pine having spine shavings are an inexpensive hydroponic growing media as properly, and plenty of business growers use it. Normally for big-scale hydroponic drip irrigation structures. Do not confuse pine shavings with saw dirt. Sawdust turns into compact and waterlogged without problems. You will need to make certain your pine shavings had been crafted from kiln-dried timber and do "now not" contain any chemical fungicides.

Kiln dried to burn off all the sap in the wood that is awful for the plant life. Maximum pine shaving merchandise might be kiln-dried to start with. Desirable supply to discover pine shavings is puppy delivery shops. It is used for such things as hamster and rabbit bedding. Just ensure to read the package to make sure it would not have any chemical additives like fungicides or scent inhibitors. You have to be best if it states it is organic.

Every other accurate cheap source for pine shavings is at feed stores, it is also used as bedding in horse stalls, and they sell it by way of a cubic yard. When you have a preference, get the most important partial size you may.

The bigger the air pockets between the shavings, the higher aeration in your roots. Pine shavings are a timber product so that they take in the water effortlessly, as a consequence, can become waterlogged effortlessly. So ensure you have suitable drainage, so the shavings do not sit in water.

If there may be an opportunity of it sitting in water, a layer of rocks at the bottom will provide useful resource drainage greatly.

COMPOSTED AND ELDERLY PINE BARK

Pine bark pine bark is one of the first growing media utilized in hydroponics. It turned into normally taken into consideration a waste product, but has determined makes use of as a ground mulch, in addition to the substrate for hydroponically grown vegetation. Pine bark is taken into consideration higher than other sorts of tree bark because it resists decomposition better, and has much less natural acids which could leach into the nutrient solution than others. The bark is typically referred to as both fresh, composted, or aged. Clean bark makes use of up greater nitrogen as it begins to decompose, so commercial growers commonly compensate by including greater nitrogen to the nutrient solution. In the course of the composting method, nitrogen is introduced to the bark and mixing it in while breaks down. So nitrogen problems are ways much less of a difficulty with composted pine bark. Aging is a comparable procedure but has less nitrogen introduced to it, so it is better than the use of sparkling bark, however now not as clean as the composted bark.

POLY (POLYURETHANE) FOAM INSULATION

Polyfoam isn't normally used in hydroponics, and hydroponics shops don't deliver it. However, it has been used as an opportunity for the use of Rockwool or oasis cubes as starter cubes with superb consequences. Polyfoam is reasonably-priced and clean to locate. Any hobby shop or region that sells fabrics must deliver it. It is most commonly used as furnishings foam, and is also referred to as "foam batting." It is available in sheets or rolls of various sizes and thicknesses. You may make your starter cubes for about one penny every using the polyfoam in case you get the one or inch thick sheets/rolls and cut them into cubes.

WATER SOAKING UP CRYSTALS (WATER-ABSORBING POLYMERS)

Water absorbing crystals water soaking up polymer crystals had been around for quite a while and are used in lots of enterprises. The entirety from baby diapers to the sports activities industry in which they're used in material rags they can wear on the top or neck to preserve cool. They are also used in gardening in which the crystals are combined into the soil to help retain moisture in the soil. Florists use them in vases to preserve plants clean, and the colored ones make for a pleasant adorned show. The crystals make bigger to typically their length as they absorb water. One pound of the crystals can keep as a whole lot as 50 gallons of water. The crystals come in many sizes, everything from powder to marble and even golf ball size. Relying on the dimensions of the crystals, they can take extra than an hour or two to absolutely absorb. While they may be full of water, the appearance and sense like a glob of jello.

The water soaking up polymer crystals are not a not unusual hydroponic developing media, but like the entirety else, it's developing in popularity. Often due to their multiplied availability. They are pretty less expensive and reusable. However, used alone with the aid of themselves, they don't permit the roots to get lots of oxygen/air. Being like jello, they p.C. Together and fill the air wallet. The larger size crystals are higher ideal to be used in hydroponics. The more significant length allows maintaining some of the air wallets among the crystals. Additionally, by way of mixing some river rock or different comparable developing media with the crystals will assist increase the air pockets among the crystals. The use of the polymer crystals for hydroponics permits for some of the most straightforward hydroponic gadget designs. Even on the slimmest of budgets. Soaking some water soaking up crystals in nutrient solution, then placing them in a field and setting your seedling's in it, you have got a hydroponically grown plant. You don't want any pumps. Just ensure there are holes in the bottom of your field, and only vicinity your field in nutrient answer a couple of times every week to re-hydrate the crystals. You may not find water soaking up polymer crystals in hydroponic stores, but they are smooth to discover. Because of their reputation, most massive nursery's bring them as soil amendments.

SAND

SandSand Is simply a growing viral media used in hydroponics. It's the main organic media used on the Epcot center Hydroponic Greenhouse in Florida. Mainly for their massive hydroponically grown vegetation and bushes. Sand is like rock, just smaller in length. Because the particle length is shorter than ordinary rock, moisture does not drain out as rapid. Sand is also usually blended with Vermiculite, Perlite, and or coco coir. All help keep moisture, too, to assist aerate the combination for the roots. While the use of sand as a growing medium, you will need to use the most significant grain length you could get. So one can assist growth aeration to the roots by growing the size of the air wallet among the grains of sand. Blending Vermiculite, Perlite, and or coco coir with the sand will even help aerate. You may also want to rinse the sand well earlier than use to get as a great deal of the dirt debris out of it as you can. One huge downside to the usage of sand as a growing medium for hydroponics is that it is cumbersome. 3-4 gallons of wet sand can weigh as much as 50lbs. So you might not want to be shifting it when you get it set up. Or use it in a ratio of something like 20%-30% sand and the relaxation Vermiculite, Perlite, or another sort of growing media to reduce weight.

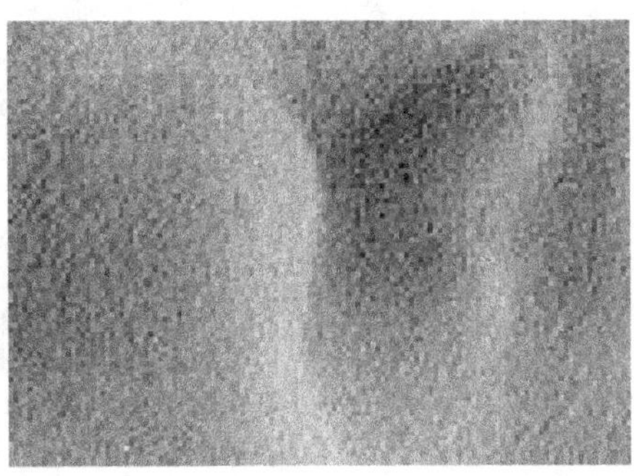

RICE HULLS

Rice hulls Depending on your area, and rice hulls may be comfortably available. It's a byproduct of the rice enterprise. Even though they're an organic plant cloth, they spoil down very slowly like coco coir, making them appropriate as a growing medium for hydroponics. Rice hulls are referred to as both sparkling, elderly, composted and parboiled, or carbonized. Fresh rice hulls are generally avoided as a hydroponic growing media because of the high possibility of contaminants inclusive of rice, fungal spores, bacteria, decaying insects, and weed seeds. Parboiled rice hulls (PRH) is carried out by using stemming and drying the rice hulls after the rice has been milled from them. This kills any spores, bacteria, and microorganisms, leaving a sterile and natural product. Rice hulls are also regularly used as a part of a combination of developing media such as 30%-40% rice hulls and pine bark blend. The general pH of parboiled and composted rice hulls ranges from 5.7 to 6.5, which is right within the pH variety for maximum hydroponically grown flora. Fresh and composted rice hulls generally tend to have excessive Manganese (Mn) content. However, troubles with Manganese toxicity can be avoided as long as the pH is above 5.

Chapter 8

Benefits Of Hydroponic Gardening

NO SOILS NEEDED

In a feel, you can develop plants in locations in which the land is confined, doesn't exist, or is heavily infected. Inside the Forties, Hydroponics becomes efficaciously used to deliver fresh veggies for troops in Wake Island, a refueling stop for Pan American airlines. This is far off arable vicinity in the Pacific Ocean. Additionally, Hydroponics has been considered as the farming of the future to develop foods for astronauts within the space (where there's no soil) using NASA.

MAKE BETTER USE OF SPACE AND LOCATION

Because all that vegetation need is provided and maintained in a machine, you may develop for your small apartment or the spare bedrooms as long as you have a few areas. Plants' roots usually enlarge and spread out looking for meals, and oxygen within the soil. This isn't always the case in hydroponics, where the roots are sunk in a tank complete of oxygenated nutrient solution and immediately touch with crucial minerals. This means you can grow your vegetation tons closer, and therefore huge area financial savings.

CLIMATE CONTROL

Like in greenhouses, hydroponic growers may have total control over the weather - temperature, humidity, mild intensification, the composition of the air. On this feel, you may develop ingredients all year round irrespective of the season. Farmers can produce foods at the right time to maximize their business profits.

HYDROPONICS IS WATER-SAVING

Plantlife grown hydroponically can use only 10% of the water in comparison to area-grown ones. In this method, water is recalculated. Plants will soak up the vital liquid, while run-off ones will be captured and return to the gadget. Water loss most effective happens in two bureaucracy - evaporation and leaks from the system (however, an efficient hydroponic setup will minimize or don't have any leaks). It's miles predicted that agriculture uses up to 80% water of the ground and floor water in the US. While water turns into a crucial issue in the future while meal production is predicted to grow by way of 70% in line with the FAQ, Hydroponics is considered a feasible way to large-scale meals manufacturing.

EFFECTIVE USE OF NUTRIENTS

In Hydroponics, you've got a hundred% to manipulate of the vitamins (foods) that plant life wants. Earlier than planting, growers can take a look at what vegetation require and the precise quantities of nutrients needed at specific tiers and blend them with water for that reason. Nutrients are conserved in the tank, so there are no losses or adjustments of nutrients like they are in the soil.

PH CONTROL OF THE SOLUTION

All the minerals are contained inside the water. That means you could earn a degree and regulate the pH ranges of your water mixture lots higher without problems as compared to the soils. That ensures the choicest vitamin uptake for the plant.

BETTER GROWTH RATE

Is hydroponically plant grown faster than in soil? Sure, it is. You're your very own boss that instructions the whole surroundings in your plant life' increase - temperature, lights, moisture, and particularly vitamins. Plantlife is placed in ideal situations, while nutrients are furnished on sufficient amounts and come into direct contact with the root structures. Thereby, plant no longer waste treasured strength looking for diluted nutrients within the soil. As an alternative, they shift all in their recognition of growing and generating culmination.

NO WEEDS

When you have grown within the soil, you may apprehend how anxious weeds purpose in your garden. It is one of the most time-ingesting duties for gardeners - till, plow, hoe, and so forth. Plants are primarily associated with the soil. So eliminate soils, and all bothers of weeds are gone.

FEWER PESTS & DISEASES

And prefer weeds, getting rids of soils helps make your plants less vulnerable to soil-borne pests like birds, gophers, groundhogs, and diseases like Fusarium, Pythium, and Rhizoctonia species. Also, while growing interior in a closed system, the gardeners can without difficulty take control of maximum surrounding variables.

LESS USE OF INSECTICIDE, AND HERBICIDES

Since you are the usage of no soils and at the same time as the weeds, pests, and plant illnesses are closely decreased, there are fewer chemical compounds used. This facilitates you to grow cleaner and healthier ingredients. The reduction of insecticide and herbicides is a sturdy factor of Hydroponics when the standards for contemporary life and food protection are increasingly more positioned on top.

LABOR AND TIME SAVERS

Except for spending fewer works on tilling, watering, cultivating, and fumigating weeds and pests, you experience plenty of time stored due to the fact plant' boom is established to be higher in Hydroponics. While agriculture is deliberate to be more technology-based totally, Hydroponics has a room in it.

HYDROPONICS IS A STRESS-RELIEVING HOBBY

This interest will put you lower back in touch with nature. Tired after a long working day and commute, you come to your small rental nook, it is time to lay returned the whole lot and play with your hydroponic lawn. Motives like lack of spaces are not right. You can begin fresh, tasty vegetables or essential herbs for your small closets, and enjoy the relaxing time along with your little inexperienced areas. Look like there are plenty of advantages of Hydroponics, and the image underneath seems to strive to steer you into Hydroponic growing. However, preserve studying to learn about its downsides.

Chapter 9

Hydroponic Systems And How Do They Work?

Hydroponics is the artwork of gardening without soil. Hydroponics is a Latin word meaning "running water." in the absence of soil, water is going to paintings offering nutrients, hydration, and oxygen to plant. From watermelons to jalapeños to orchids, plant life flourishes underneath the cautious routine of hydroponics. Using minimum area, 90% much less water than conventional agriculture, and imaginative layout, hydroponic gardens grow stunning fruits and plants in 1/2 the time. Although the generation sounds modern, the history of hydroponics dates lower back to the famed hanging Gardens of Babylon, one of the Seven Wonders of the ancient world.

The Euphrates River was diverted into channels that cascaded down the lavish garden partitions. In the thirteenth century, Marco Polo wrote of witnessing floating gardens in China. But, hydroponics is far from merely an innovation of the historic a while. In the Nineties, NASA grew aeroponic bean seedlings in 0 gravity aboard an area station, beginning up the opportunity of sustainable agriculture in the area. Hydroponics is still a timeless and dynamic method of water conservation and crop manufacturing.

HOW DOES HYDROPONICS WORK?

Hydroponic structures work via permitting minute control over environmental conditions like temperature and pH stability and maximized publicity to nutrients and water. Hydroponics operates underneath a straightforward principle: offer flora precisely what they need once they want it. Hydroponics administers nutrient answers tailored to the needs of the precise plant being grown. They will let you manipulate exactly how lots mild the plants get hold of and for the way lengthy. PH levels can be monitored and adjusted. In a highly customized and managed environment, plant growth quickens.

With the aid of controlling the surroundings of the plant, many hazard elements are decreased. Plants grown in gardens and fields are brought to a host of variables that negatively impact their health and boom. Fungus within the soil can unfold illnesses to vegetation. Wildlife like rabbits can plunder ripening vegetables from your lawn. Pests like locusts can descend on vegetation and obliterate them in a day. Hydroponic systems end the unpredictability of developing plant life exterior and on the earth. Without the mechanical resistance of the soil, seedlings can mature much faster. Through doing away with insecticides, hydroponics produce lots more healthy and excellent results and vegetables. Without limitations, vegetation is unfastened to develop vigorously and unexpectedly.

WHAT ARE THE COMPONENTS OF A HYDROPONIC SYSTEM?

To maintain a flourishing hydroponic system, you will need to become acquainted with a few components that make hydroponics run efficiently.

GROWING MEDIA

Hydroponic vegetation is regularly grown in inert media that help the plant's weight and anchor its root structure. Developing media is bogus for soil. However, it does not provide any independent vitamins to the plant. Alternatively, this porous media keeps moisture and vitamins from the nutrient solution, which it then provides to the plant. Many growing media are also pH-impartial, so they'll now not disillusioned the balance of your nutrient answer. There are a bunch of various media to select from, and the precise plant and hydroponic system will dictate which media high-quality suits your endeavor. Hydroponic growing media is wide to be had both online and at nearby nurseries and gardening shops.

AIR STONES AND AIR PUMPS

Plantlife that is submerged in water can quickly drown if the water isn't always sufficiently aerated. Air stones disperse tiny bubbles of dissolved oxygen in the course of your nutrient answer reservoir. These bubbles additionally help calmly distribute the dissolved nutrients within the answer. Air stones do not generate oxygen on their personal. They want to be attached to an outside air pump thru opaque food grade plastic tubing (the opacity will save you algae growth from putting in). Air stones and air pumps are popular aquarium additives and can be purchased easily at pet stores.

NET POTS

Internet pots are mesh planters that preserve hydroponic plant life. The latticed cloth allows roots to develop out of the perimeters and bottom of the container, giving extra publicity to oxygen and nutrients. Internet pots additionally offer advanced drainage as compared to conventional clay or plastic containers.

Chapter 10

Build Your Own Hydroponic Systems

Welcome to domestic Hydro structures, the area in which you'll be capable of locating information about whatever related to hydroponics, in addition to hydroponic systems and the way to construct your very own hydroponic systems. Developing vegetation correctly is not all; it's were given to be low cost too, or what is the factor. We aren't' interested in growing a $12 tomato, and we attempt to show you that you may develop higher produce at domestic hydroponically, and for less money than you could buy it for at the shop, or even grow it in the ground. After all, it would not be worthwhile if it wasn't most economical to develop them hydroponically now would it not?

Domestic made hydroponic gadget growing lettuce. You don't want a high-priced hydroponic device, luxurious nutrients, or maybe high-priced develop lighting to develop your plants hydroponically. You may build your excellent hydroponic structures inexpensively. Also, there are plenty of superb commercially made fee powerful vitamins you may use. You don't even want any develop lighting if you may make use of loose herbal daylight. It's smooth to build your hydroponic systems. Irrespective of what you want to grow, hydroponic systems, in reality, most effectively have and want some essential components to work thoroughly.

THE HYDROPONIC SYSTEM ONLY NEED A FEW ESSENTIAL PARTS TO BUILD

Growing Chamber (Or Tray),

The developing chamber is the part of the hydroponic device wherein the plant roots could be developing. Positioned, the developing chamber is the box for the basis region. This area offers plant support, as well as is in which the roots get entry to the nutrient answer. It also protects the roots from light, warmness, and pests. It's critical to preserve the root region's fresh and mild evidence. Prolonged light will damage the roots, and high temps within the root quarter will motive warmth pressure in your plants, as well as reason fruit and flower drop due to warmness strain. The nutrient answer temperature itself is an essential part of retaining the roots and whole root zone comfy for the plants. The scale and form of the growing chamber rely upon on the type of hydroponic machine your building, in addition to the kind of plant you'll be growing in it. Bigger plants have more significant root systems and want a greater area to maintain them in. The designs here are infinite. Nearly anything can be used as the developing chamber, you do not want to apply whatever made from metal, or it may corrode or react with the vitamins. If you look around, you may get lots of ideas of what and how you may effortlessly use many different things for building the developing chamber of your hydroponic system.

Reservoir,

The reservoir is the part of the hydroponic device that holds the nutrient solution. The nutrient answer consists of plant nutrients that are jumbled together water. Depending on the form of hydroponic machine, the nutrient answer can be pumped from the reservoir up to the developing chamber (root sector) in cycles the usage of a timer, in addition to always without a timer, or the roots may even hang down into the reservoir 24/7, making the reservoir the developing chamber additionally.

You may make a reservoir out of virtually anything plastic that holds water. As long as it does not leak holds enough water and is wiped clean out properly first, it can be used as a reservoir. Read this newsletter for extra approximately how big your nutrient reservoir should be. A reservoir additionally needs to be mild evidence.

If you can preserve it over your head and spotlight coming via it, it's not mild proof. But it's easy to make any light container evidence with the aid of portraying it, masking it, or wrapping something like bubble wrap insulation around it. Algae and microorganisms can start growing with even low mild stages.

Submersible Pump,

Maximum hydroponic systems use a submersible pump to pump the water (nutrient answer) from the reservoir up to the developing chamber/root quarter for the vegetation. Submersible pumps can without problems are found at hydroponic deliver save, or maximum domestic improvement stores with lawn components as a fountain and pond pumps.

They'll also come in a massive style of sizes. Examine this page for the way to decide what length pump you need in your hydroponic gadget? The submersible pumps are not anything higher than an impeller that makes use of an electromagnet to spin it.

They can also effortlessly be taken all aside to be wiped clean very well. If it doesn't come with a filter, you may without difficulty make one by using reducing a chunk of furnace filter out display screen or comparable material to healthy. You need to easy both the pump and filter regularly to hold them smooth.

Delivery System,

A hydroponic structures water/nutrient solution shipping gadget is, in reality, pretty simple, as well as extremely customizable while constructing your hydro structures. Except for the pump, it's not anything extra than simply the pluming the water/nutrient answer is going thru to get to the plant roots inside the developing chamber and lower back to the reservoir again.

Generally, the most effective and satisfactory substances to apply for the nutrient transport gadget are a combination of well-known p.C tubing and connectors, popular garden irrigation tubing and connectors, as well as blue or black vinyl tubing. Depending on the kind of hydroponic machine you build, you can need to apply drip emitters or sprayers as part of your nutrient answer delivery machine. Even as they may be beneficial, they also can clog. So in case you do, make sure you have extras you could fast swap out while you smooth the clogged ones. We strive to avoid the use of emitters because they do clog, as well as extra fee money.

SIMPLE TIMER,

Depending on the kind of hydroponic machine you construct and wherein you region the gadget to grow your plant life. You may need one or simple timers. If you use artificial lighting to develop the plant as opposed to natural sunlight, you'll want a timer to govern the on/off instances for the lights device. For flood and drain, drip, and aeroponic systems, you may wish to a timer to control the on/off situations for the submersible water pump. Some types of aeroponic structures may additionally want a unique timer. Visit the aeroponic structures page to find out extra about the forms of aeroponic systems, and timers for them. Famous everyday light timers paintings are first-class for each the lights as well as the submersible pumps. However, we do suggest making sure the timer is rated for 15 amps as opposed to 10 amps. Fifteen amp timers are frequently called heavy duty; if not, check the back of the package or timer for the 15 amp rating. Also, try to get one for outdoor use. They typically have a cowl and generally are water-proof. I don't advocate the other high priced digital timers over the analog dial kind. Surely due to the fact digital timers will lose all reminiscence, in addition to your settings, if they lose electricity or get unplugged, even for one 2d for any purpose (except you discover one with a battery backup). They frequently don't have any other real on/off settings than the analog kind as well. Just make sure the timer you get has pinned around the dial.

Air Pump,

Apart from water tradition systems, air pumps are non-obligatory in hydroponic structures. However, using them has benefits, and air pumps are extraordinarily cheaper. Air pumps may be found anywhere they sell aquarium supplies. Air pumps deliver air and oxygen to the water and roots. Air is pumped via an airline to air stones that create a gaggle of small bubbles that upward thrust up through the nutrient solution. In the waterway of life systems, the air pump helps keep the plant roots from suffocating even as they submerged inside the nutrient solution 24/7. For any other form of hydroponic machine, the air pump is usually used within the reservoir. It facilitates to increase dissolved oxygen tiers in the water up and preserve the water oxygenated. Go to this web page for higher, approximately dissolved oxygen stages. Different benefits of the use of air pumps are that because the air bubbles upward thrust, they maintain the water and nutrients moving and circulating; this continues the vitamins lightly blended all of the time. The circulating oxygenated water also enables pathogens from gaining a foothold inside the reservoir.

Grow Lights,

Grow lighting is an optional part of hydroponic systems. Depending on wherein you propose to position your hydroponic gadget, and develop your plant. You may pick out to both use herbal sunlight and artificial mild to grow your plants with. If you may employ it, we select natural daylight, and it's is free and would not require any more equipment. However, if there isn't always enough herbal daylight wherein you placed your hydroponic system, or at that time of yr, you will want to use as a minimum a few artificial mild to grow your plant. Develop lights are exceptional than most trendy family lighting. Develop lighting fixtures are designed to emit positive shade spectrums that mimic natural sunlight. The vegetation uses those color spectrums (wavelengths) of light to behavior photosynthesis. The plants want to behavior photosynthesis so that you can grow and convey fruit and plant. So the kind, as well as the quantity of light a plant gets, will significantly affect the vegetation ability to photosynthesize and accordingly, grow. Visit our page on lighting and develop lighting for hydroponic plant life for extra about the distinct sorts of artificial lighting fixtures used to grow plant life.

Chapter 11

Clarification Of Understandings Of

Different Types Of Hydroponic Gardens

CLARIFICATION OF UNDERSTANDINGS OF DIFFERENT TYPES OF HYDROPONIC GARDENS

There are six fundamental varieties of hydroponic structures to choose from:

- Wick Systems

- Deep Water Culture (DWC)

- Nutrient Film Technique (NFT).

- Ebb and Flow (Flood and Drain)

- Aeroponics

- Drip Systems

There are six main types of hydroponic systems to choose from:

- Wick Systems

- Deep Water Culture (DWC)

- Nutrient Film Technique (NFT).

- Ebb and Flow (Flood and Drain)

- Aeroponics

- Drip Systems

Wicking Systems

A wicking device is the maximum fundamental form of hydro system you may build. It's been used for heaps of years, even though it wasn't taken into consideration a hydroponic machine lower back then.

It's what's called passive hydroponics, meaning that you don't want any air pumps or water pumps to apply it. Nutrients and water are moved right into a plant's root quarter through a wick that is regularly something as easy as a rope or piece of felt. One key to fulfillment with a wicking gadget is to use a developing media that transports water and vitamins correctly. Correct alternatives consist of coconut coir, perlite, or vermiculite. Wick structures are accurate for smaller flora that don't expend loads of water or nutrients. A large plant can also have a hard time getting sufficient of both through a secure wick system.

Blessings of Wick structures

- Truly "hands-off" in case you set it up efficaciously

- tremendous for small plant, amateur gardeners, and children

Downsides of Wick structures

- no longer excellent for more abundant vegetation

- incorrect wick placement or cloth can mean loss of life for your vegetation

Deep Water Culture (Dwc) Systems

In a DWC machine, you use a reservoir to keep a nutrient solution. The roots of your plant life are suspended in that answer, so they get a steady delivery of water, oxygen, and nutrients.

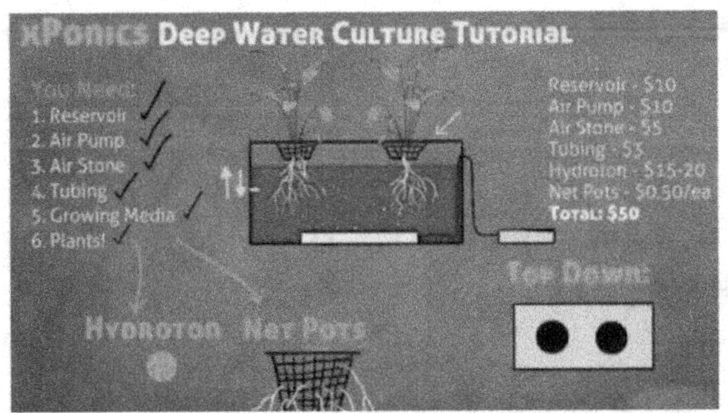

To oxygenate the water, you operate an air pump with an air stone to pump bubbles into the nutrient solution. This prevents your roots from drowning inside the water — a weird element to think about. However, it can (and does) show up to many novice hydroponic gardeners. Your plant life is commonly housed in internet pots, which might be placed in foam board or into the pinnacle of the container that you're using in your reservoir. With a few hydroponic developing media introduced into your internet pots, they offer a domestic for the very beginning of your root device and plant stems.

Advantages of Deep Water lifestyle

- Very less expensive and easy to make at home

- extremely low-upkeep

- Recirculating, so less wasted inputs

Downsides of Deep Water culture

- Does no longer paintings properly for massive plant life

- Does not paintings properly for a plant with long-developing duration

Nutrient Film Technique (Nft) Systems

Plants are grown in channels that have a nutrient solution pumping through them and continue running along the bottom of the chain. When the solution reaches the end of the channel, it drops back into the main reservoir and is sent back to the beginning of the system again. This makes it a recirculating system, just like a deep water culture.

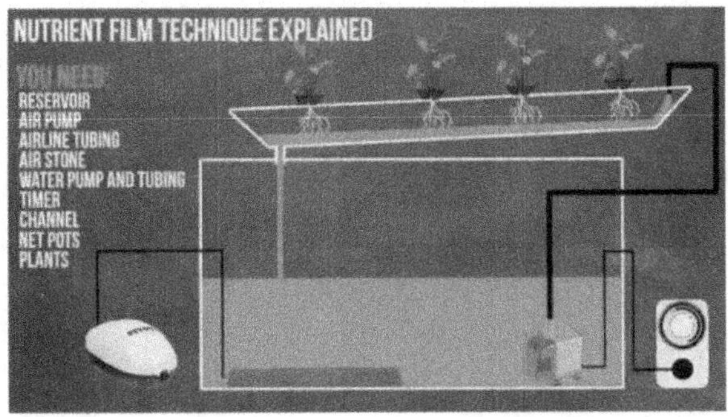

Unlike deep water culture, your plants roots are not completely submerged in an NFT system — hence the "film" part of the system's name. Plants are placed in these channels using net pots and growing medium and can be replaced or harvested on a one-by-one basis.

Benefits of Nutrient Film Technique

- Minimal growing medium needed

- The recirculating system means less waste

Downsides of Nutrient Film Technique

- Pump failure of any kind can completely ruin your crop

- Roots can become overgrown and clog the channels

Ebb And Flow / Flood And Drain Systems

Ebb and drift structures that are also known through the name Flood and Drain are a less-generally visible system. However, they're nevertheless pretty useful and can be the great desire relying on your situation.

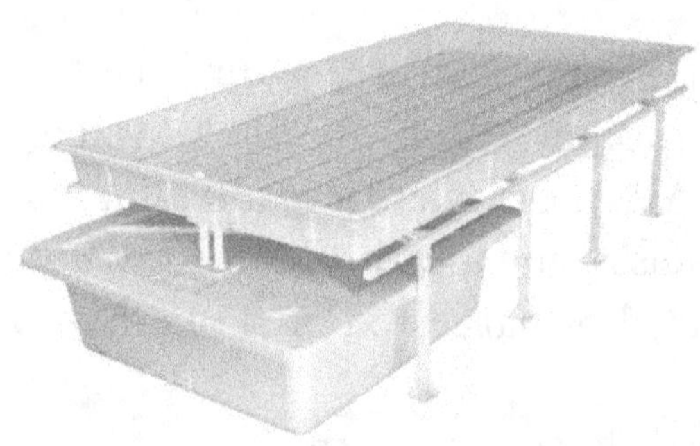

Not like the previous hydro systems we've got protected, an ebb and float gadget does not reveal the roots of your flora to a nutrient solution always. Instead, you grow in a tray packed with a growing medium. The tray is "flooded" along with your nutrient solution a few instances in line with day, depending on factors like:

- The scale of your plant

- The water requirement of your flora

- The air temperature

- Where your vegetation are in their boom cycle

and plenty of more Flooding is executed by the use of a reservoir beneath the tray, a water pump, and a time to schedule the flooding cycle. After the tray is flooded, gravity drains the solution backtrack into the reservoir, where it is being oxygenated with the aid of an air pump and air stone. It sits there watching for the next flood cycle, and the manner goes on. Hydroponic growers pick ebb and glide systems for their flexibility. Most of them will fill the tray with a developing medium of their choice and additionally add net pots to prepare their flora and manipulate the roots a bit extra.

Advantages of Ebb and flow

- green use of water and energy

- noticeably customizable for your particular needs

Downsides of Ebb and glide

- Roots can dry out quickly if environmental situations are off or the pump or timer fails

- uses quite a few developing media

Aeroponics Systems

Aeroponic structures are the maximum "excessive-tech" hydroponic setups that you can construct. However, they're no longer that complex when you understand how they paintings. An aeroponic device is similar to an NFT gadget in that the roots are usually suspended in the air. The difference is that an aeroponic machine achieves this with the aid of misting the root sector with a nutrient solution continuously in place of walking a thin film of nutrient answer along a channel.

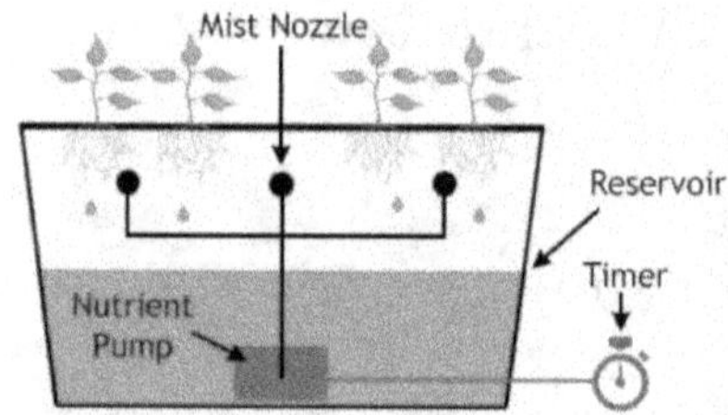

Some growers favor misting on a cycle like an ebb and float gadget. However, the period is a lot shorter, typically most effective, waiting a couple of minutes among every misting. It's also feasible to mist on a persistent foundation and use a finer sprayer to ensure more oxygen receives to the central region.

Aeroponic structures had been proven to develop plants even quicker than some of the simpler structures like deep water lifestyle. However, this has not been demonstrated to be true in all cases. If you need to test with this gadget, you'll want specialized spray nozzles to atomize the nutrient answer.

Advantages of Aeroponics

- Roots frequently are uncovered to more oxygen than submerged-root structures

Downsides of Aeroponics

- high-stress nozzles can fail, and roots can dry out

- now not as cheap or clean to installation as different strategies

Drip Systems

Drip systems are extraordinarily not unusual in business operations, but less not unique in leisure gardens. That is due to the fact they're simple to function a vast scale but barely overkill for a smaller lawn. Regardless, they're a super way to develop hydroponically, which you ought to remember.

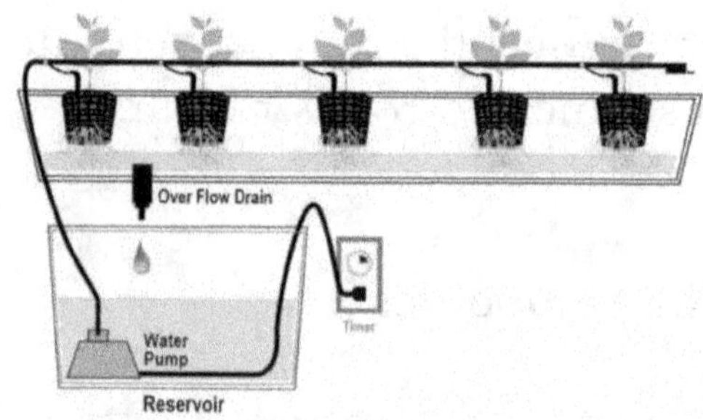

Advantages of Drip structures

- high degree of manipulating over feeding and watering schedule

- less likely to interrupt

- particularly cheap

Downsides of Drip structures

- maybe overkill for a smaller garden

- Fluctuating pH and nutrient ranges (if the usage of the recirculating machine)

- excessive waste (if the use of waste gadget)

Chapter 12

Greenhouse And Greenhouse Lightning

GREENHOUSE

Greenhouse, also called a glasshouse, a building designed for the protection of smooth or out-of-season plants against immoderate cold or warmness. Within the seventeenth century, greenhouses have been a regular brick or timber shelters with a standard proportion of window space and some method of heating. As glass has become cheaper and as more state-of-the-art styles of heating became to be had, the greenhouse developed into a roofed and walled structure constructed of glass with a minimal wood or metallic skeleton. By way of the middle of the 19th century, the greenhouse had evolved from an insignificant haven from a hostile climate into managed surroundings, adapted to the needs of particular plants. A massive boom inside the availability of individual vegetation inside the nineteenth century brought about a substantial growth in the glasshouse way of life in England and someplace else. Massive greenhouses are vital in agriculture and horticulture and for horticultural technological know-how, while smaller structures are generally utilized by hobbyists, collectors, and domestic gardeners.

The cutting-edge greenhouse is often a glass- or plastic-enclosed framed structure that is used for the production of fruits, vegetables, plants, and every other flora that require unique situations of temperature. The fundamental structural bureaucracy is the span-kind greenhouse, which has a double-sloped, or A-formed roof, and the lean-to greenhouse, which has the handiest one roof slope and leans towards the aspect of a constructing. Or other span-type greenhouses are now and then joined facet by facet so that they have fewer external walls, and heating prices are therefore less. A greenhouse has a massive expanse of glazing on its aspects and roof so that the plants are exposed to herbal mild for a whole lot of the day. Glass has been the traditional glazing cloth, but plastic movies, which include polyethylene or polyvinyl, and fiberglass are also common. The framing of the shape is manufactured from aluminum, galvanized steel, or such woods as redwood, cedar, or cypress. A greenhouse is heated partially by way of the rays of the sun and partially by artificial approaches, such as circulating steam, hot water, or warm air. Because a greenhouse can turn out to be too hot in addition to too bloodless, a few sorts of ventilating device is also wanted; this consists typically of roof openings, which may be operated routinely or automatically, and cease-wall openings, through which electric powered fanatics draw air and flow into it at some point of the indoors.

The plant life grown in greenhouses falls into numerous broad categories based totally on their temperature necessities at some point in nighttime hours. In a groovy greenhouse, the midnight temperature falls to approximately 7–10 °C (forty-five –50 °F). Most of the vegetation proper to chill greenhouses are azaleas, itineraries, cyclamens, carnations, fuchsias, geraniums, sweet peas, snapdragons, and a variety of bulbous vegetation along with daffodils, irises, tulips, hyacinths, and narcissi. A heated greenhouse has midnight temperatures of 10–13 °C (50–55 °F). Begonias, gloxinias, African violets, chrysanthemums, orchids, roses, coleuses, and lots of forms of ferns and cacti and different succulents are suited to such temperatures. In a tropical greenhouse, or hothouse, which has nighttime temperatures of sixteen–21 °C (60–70 °F), caladiums, philodendrons, gardenias, poinsettias, bougainvilleas, passion plant, and plenty of styles of arms and orchids may be grown. In international locations with cold climates, commercial greenhouses are used to grow tomatoes and other heat-weather veggies. See also a conservatory.

Understanding Greenhouse Lighting

There are loads greater to greenhouse lighting fixtures than meets the eye. Growers in search of the right lighting for their greenhouse need to recall the following three factors: the sort of crop being grown, what time of yr its miles, and what sort of daylight is available? Greenhouses usually require six hours of direct or complete spectrum mild each day. If this may be performed clearly, supplemental lighting has to be incorporated. Supplemental lighting fixtures are using multiple, high-depth synthetic lighting fixtures to sell crop boom and yield. Hobbyists like to apply them to maintain boom and increase the growing season, while business growers use them to boost yields and profits. Equally essential as supplemental lighting fixtures is photoperiod manipulate lights. A photoperiod of light is the wide variety of hours that a plant receives light in 24 hours. As an example, if the sun rises at 6 in the morning and units at 8 in the night, a 14-hour photoperiod has lapsed. Photoperiod manipulates lighting fixtures are used to simulate lengthy days, triggering early flowering or promoting behind schedule flowering, depending on the plant's desires. Growers have a big selection of lights options to pick from, so it's crucial to apprehend the nuances of differing lights styles. Permit's examine the makes use of and advantages of four different lights sorts.

HIGH-PRESSURE SODIUM FIXTURES

High-pressure sodium furniture offers more orange and pink spectrum mild and features a golden-white look to the human eye. On account that they sell budding and flowering, they are normally used later in the boom cycle of the plant. These fixtures are approximately seven times greener than incandescent bulbs and work great while used in conjunction with natural sunlight hours, making them a high-quality alternative for greenhouses. Excessive strain sodium lighting fixtures additionally offer the capability for a 10% increase in intensity, and photosynthetically lively radiation (PAR.) give high-stress sodium lighting fixtures approximately four to 5 mins to warm up and one minute to cool down. Its miles for this reason that they aren't correct for locations in which the lighting fixtures activate and off frequently. It's also vital to be cognizant of placement; excessive pressure sodium lighting fixtures should be hooked up 30 to 36 inches above the plant for the highest quality consequences.

FIXED AND PROGRAMMABLE SPECTRUM LED FIXTURES

LED (mild emitting diode) furniture is the longest lasting option offered by way of Growers deliver, with an average lifespan of 50,000 hours. The diode of an LED gained burns out as fast as popular mild bulbs, which gives it such an incredibly long lifespan. LED lighting fixtures have a higher performance than widespread lighting fixtures due to the fact more of the energy input goes to light than heat. For example, incandescent bulbs are handiest about 20% green, as maximum in their input electricity is going to generating warmness. Possibly one of the most important advantages of LED lighting fixtures is the huge electricity savings. They're effortlessly incorporated into any operation and offer up to 70% savings when compared to high-depth discharge (hid) lighting. There is no warm-up time required with an LED fixture, and they're also free of mercury, making disposal an awful lot less difficult than different bulbs. LED's offer advanced functionality when used as a sole source of lighting, making them an attractive choice for many growers.

CERAMIC METAL HALIDE

Ceramic, metallic halide lamps are used for their blue mild, even though they appear shiny-white to the human eye. They could easily characteristic as a number one light source, with a mean lifespan among 8,000 to 50, 000 hours. On account, those metallic halides are 3 to five instances greener than incandescent bulbs. They make a first-rate choice for areas that don't receive herbal sun. Crucial to observe is that steel halides should heat up for about 5 mins or less before they could deliver out completely mild.

Additionally, they need a cool down duration of approximately five to 10 mins earlier than restarting. Because of this, they may now be not recommended for places where the lighting fixtures will activate and off regularly. Ceramic steel halide lights have to be hung 30 to 36 inches over vegetation and may bring about darkened leaves and typical healthy-looking greenery. Growers deliver PARLucent Ceramic, metallic Halide lighting fixtures that are ideal for greenhouse and hydroponic programs. Growers often use them inside the early segment of a plant's life when seeds are within the vegetative boom segment. The dimmable ballast lets in growers to attain the suitable lighting for their operation. They're silent too, so there aren't any bothersome humming, humming, or excessive-pitched noises to cope with.

T5 FIXTURES

T5 furnishings are the maximum efficiency and maximum famous fluorescent greenhouse lighting fixtures option for developing. They use less electricity than conventional lamps and may last as long as 50,000 hours. These environmentally-pleasant lighting fixtures now and then characteristic aluminum reflectors for optimum efficiency. They may be perfect for use in hydroponics, greenhouses, warehouses, and barns and greater. They may be used from the initial segment of a seed beginning to complete the period increase. The letter "T" denotes the tubular form of the lamp, and the variety five shows its diameter in eighths of an inch. T5 lamps are slim, simplest 5/eight" of an inch in diameter, which makes T5 fluorescent tubes greener than general fluorescent tubes.GrowSpan's high-performance forty-five" T5 Fluorescent Lamp functions extremely excessive lumen output and full-spectrum lighting fixtures that are top-notch for vegetation from the seedling degree up to full term boom. Its minimum warmth output way that it can accurately be placed very near plant life, within 6 to twelve inches to be unique. While there's technically no such element as an excessive amount of light, it's critical no longer to use too effective a light in a small space, that can bring about overheating of the leaf floor location. With so many greenhouse light options tailor-made to unique plant sorts and ranges of boom, it's easy to look at why professional steering is so valued using growers anywhere.

While working with Grow Span, growers have to get entry to custom lighting fixtures plans, computerized and computer-managed lights, or even Greenhouse specialists that offer expert lighting layout. Grow Span's wide variety of lighting solutions, from supplemental growth to photoperiod manipulate, make optimizing a grow area an easy, green process.

Chapter 13

Choosing The Right Hydroponic System

HYDROPONIC SYSTEMS & WHAT'S RIGHT FOR YOU

If you've been considering a hydroponic device to your garden, you'll be feeling beaten with the variety of alternatives available to you. In this text, we'll clarify and outline each of the top six hydroponic structures so you can choose the precise answer for your garden.

HYDROPONICS

"Hydroponics" refers to a soil-much less growing gadget at either a business or residential level. Those structures assist plant life development by using presenting water and vitamins through a non-soil growing medium. Typical growing media encompass:

- Vermiculite

- Perlite

- Coconut coir

- Rockwool/stone wool

- Clay pellets

- Sand/gravel/sawdust

- Peat moss

Hydroponics removes the barriers among the plant and its vitamins. This affords the roots with direct access to water, oxygen, and nutrients that it desires to grow and survive. Due to the fact, there's no soil, and there may be additionally no want for dangerous pesticides or chemicals. There's also a decrease in the danger of plant disease or exposure to outside elements. There are six essential styles of hydroponic systems to recollect in your garden: wicking, deep water subculture (DWC), nutrient movie method (NFT), ebb and glide, aeroponics, and drip structures.

WICKING SYSTEMS

The wick machine is the maximum fundamental sort of hydroponic manner, also known as "the training wheels of the hydroponic world." This type of boom has been used for hundreds of years, even before the period "hydroponic" became considered. This is the form of device you'll see in youngsters' science classes. In a wick system, the vitamins and water are transported to the plant' roots the usage of a wick, like a rope or a bit of felt. The vegetation is suspended in some growing medium, like coconut coir or perlite. Underneath the developing tank is a reservoir of water and nutrient solutions. One cease of the wick is inside the solution, and the opposite cease of the wick is inside the growing media. This allows the wick to move the water and nutrients at the identical fee that the plant life's roots require the vitamins. Every time the roots are equipped to take in, they'll take within the nutrients from the wick. Wick structures are "passive hydroponics" because they don't require air or water pumps. This makes them low-fee and smooth to hold, particularly for novice growers.

Pros:

- The wick machine is incredible for smaller plant life.

- As soon as carried out, it's a smooth and arms-off developing manner.

- It's a terrific alternative for novices or kids gardeners.

- Wick is one of the lowest value structures to implement.

Cons:

- Wicking isn't powerful for large plants or sizeable gardens.

- Failure to set up well or hold the integrity of the wick can kill the vegetation.

You want:

- Reservoir

- growing medium

- Wick

- reveal structures

- Nutrient solutions

- Distilled water

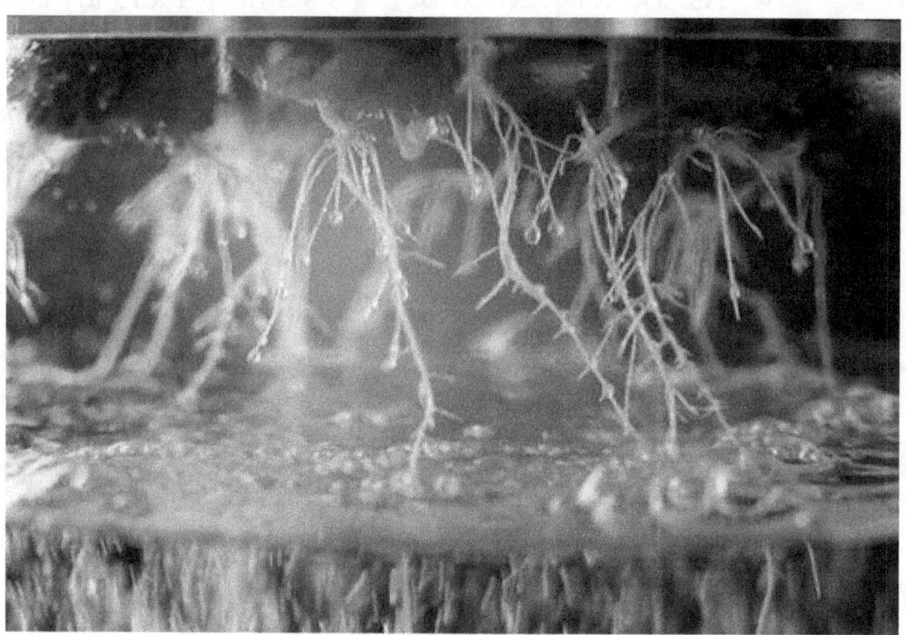

DEEP WATER CULTURE (DWC)

The deepwater tradition (DWC) is the perfect device to keep for maximum growers. A DWC includes a reservoir filled with water and nutrient solution. The plants are suspended over the reservoir the usage of an internet pot and growing media. The roots themselves are submerged within the reservoir so that they have a regular supply of water and nutrients. Plant roots want oxygen, or they can "drown." as a result, you need to use an air pump with an air stone to pump bubbles in the reservoir to continuously oxygenate the water and deliver vital oxygen to the roots.

Pros:

- DWC is less expensive and coffee-price to hold.

- Protection is low and simplest calls for a reservoir, suspension system, and primary air pumps.

- It's a recirculating procedure, which means that much less waste and extra value savings.

Cons:

- DWC doesn't commonly work for larger plants or people with an extended growing duration.

- If no longer well managed, plant roots can suffocate in solution.

You want:

- Reservoir

- internet pots

- growing medium

- Air pump & air stone

- Nutrient answer

- Distilled water

NUTRIENT FILM TECHNIQUE (NFT)

The nutrient movie technique (NFT) components the plants' roots with a skinny movie of nutrients. The water and nutrient answer is held in a massive reservoir, which has an air pump and air stone to live oxygenated (like a DWC device). But, in contrast to the submerged roots of a DWC, the NFT-machine plant is grown in a close-by channel (in net pots).A water pump, set on a timer, pushes water through the channel. This provides a skinny movie of nutrients and water to the plant life, in which the roots are not completely submerged. At the quit of the channel, the solution drops lower back into the main reservoir to be reused within the system.

Pros:

- NFT is a low-waste recirculating machine.

- The movie ensures you don't suffocate your roots.

- There's minimum to no growing media wanted.

Cons:

- A malfunction in the pumps can damage the crop.

- Roots can overgrow and intertwine alongside the channel.

- The recirculating system can clog the pipes and channels if the water isn't properly balanced.

You want:

- Reservoir

- Air pump & air stone

- Plant channel

- Water pump

- Timer

- internet pots

- Nutrient answer

- Distilled water

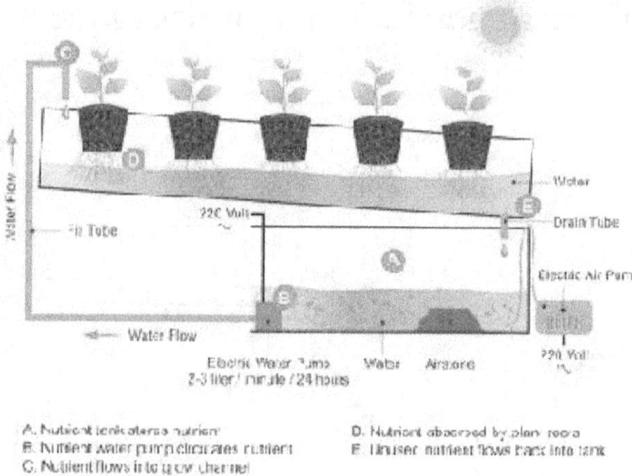

EBB AND FLOW

An ebb and drift device, also called "flood and drain," floods your plants with nutrients on a cycle. That is a less common practice because it's not as flexible for your vegetation's needs. A few growers like this machine, though, as it doesn't constantly reveal the plant roots to the nutrient answer. You fill a tray with a growing medium to residence the plant. A timed pump will "flood" the tray with nutrient solution on a cyclic schedule. The cycle of flooding relies upon on the kind of plant, water testing, the air temperature, the growth cycle, and extra. After flooding the tray, gravity drains the solution lower back into the reservoir to be reused. An air pump has to oxygenate the water in the reservoir because it waits for the following flood cycle.

This gadget can work nicely if you have strong monitoring approaches to understand your plant's boom consumption of nutrients.

Pros:

An ebb and flow machine doesn't expose your plant to steady water. This can help enhance increase and yield if it should be cycled. Ebb and float are recirculating systems that are green use of water and strength.

Cons:

- If no longer balanced or timed properly, the machine may additionally over-saturate your plants or dry them out.

  - Ebb and flow require steady tracking, especially of environmental elements like water pH.

You need:

- Reservoir
- Tray
- developing medium
- Water pump
- Timer
- Air pump
- Nutrient answer
- Distilled water

AEROPONICS

Aeroponic systems are the maximum high-tech and generally extra expensive, but they're additionally one of the handiest systems. In an aeroponic machine, the plant life and roots are suspended in the air. The reservoir (with oxygenating air pump) has misters, which spray a great spray over the plant roots. Some growers will use a nonstop, fine mist even as others will mist on a cycle. The cycle of misting is shorter than the flood and drain version, with only some mins among each cycle. This allows the roots to have nutrients without oversaturation or submersion continuously. It additionally evidently allows the roots more exposure to oxygen, which is important for boom and improvement.

Pros:

- The roots are exposed to greater oxygen.

- there may be much less likelihood of oversaturation or underneath-saturation of roots.

- Aeroponic systems are normally the very best to hold and display.

Cons:

- That is one of the more pricey systems.

- A failure of a pump or mist nozzle could have dire results on plants.

You need:

- Reservoir
- Air pump
- Timer
- Suspension pots
- Mist nozzles
- Timer
- Nutrient answer
- Distilled water

DRIP SYSTEMS

Drip systems are usually found in commercial settings as opposed to residential because they're better implemented on a large scale. These are similar to NFT systems, where the plants are held in a separate channel. The plants are suspended in net pots over a thin layer of water and nutrient solution. A pump continuously moves the water throughout the channel to improve oxygenation and nutrient uptake. The leftover solution flows back into the reservoir to be reused.

Pros:

- Drip systems offer greater control over the schedule of feeding.

- For commercial spaces, these can be inexpensive and highly effective.

Cons:

- These systems require a lot of moving parts, which could be overkill for home gardens.

- You have to be highly aware of monitoring pH and nutrient levels.

- These don't recirculate all solutions, which can lead to a high level of waste.

You Need:

- Reservoir

- Water pump

- Timer

- Net pots

- Growing medium

- Channel

- Pump system

- Nutrient solution

- Distilled water

- The Bottom Line

Choosing the right system is critical to your hydroponic gardening success. If you want something low-cost and relatively low-maintenance, especially for new growers, consider a wicking system, DWC, or NFT. If you are a more advanced grower looking for greater yield with stronger monitoring processes, consider ebb and flow or aeroponics. There are several variables to consider when choosing your hydroponic system. From price to plants to waste, it's important to research the perfect hydroponics system for your garden.

Chapter 14

Starting A Hydroponics Business

HOW TO START A HYDROPONIC FARM BUSINESS

A hydroponic farm business grows and sells plant life, veggies, grass, and different styles of greenery to organizations and people. Examples of such groups include grocery stores and eating places. The twist to this fashion of enterprise is water solvent is used to develop the plant in preference to the soil. Hydroponic farm businesses are normally positioned interior. Commonly, those indoor environments are greenhouses. This commercial enterprise is a first-rate manner to offer again to the community. Hydroponic farm commercial enterprise proprietors provide people with the first-rate, nutritious, and tasty produce. Those businesses also develop lovable plant life and other sorts of greenery that beautify the local people. Furthermore, hydroponic farm agencies benefit the nearby surroundings as they are environmentally-pleasant in comparison to conventional techniques of farming. Earlier than we inform you about the basics of beginning a hydroponics enterprise, allow us to study what the commercial enterprise entails. Hydroponic farming involves promoting vegetation, vegetables, and other homegrown products to various individuals and companies like grocery shops. But, rather than developing the plants in the soil they're grown on water. Those farms are by, and large indoor farms, and broadly speaking, natural vegetables are grown. These days, millennials choose ingesting organically grown meals, so the enterprise of hydroponic farming is thriving around the world. People may even develop a lot of their preferred vegetation right in their very own home, and all this is wished is the right developing equipment to begin. That is making it famous among many owners across the world who do now not have to get entry to a garden. If you are trying to start a hydroponics business even though there are some belongings, you should realize approximately first.

TIPS TO STARTING A HYDROPONICS BUSINESS

We've compiled some essential steps for beginning your own hydroponic farming business. They are easy but vital in case you need to start your commercial enterprise without plenty of problems.

PLAN WHAT YOU WANT TO DO

It's far crucial to devise what you want to do together with your enterprise. Determine out your costs and what sort of you need to make investments. Make a mental calculation of the duration in which you want to break even. This can help you live heading in the right direction. It's miles usually better to have matters planned thoroughly in preference to halfheartedly and figuring out your errors halfway through building your commercial enterprise.

LEGALIZE YOUR BUSINESS ENTITY

The most important part of forming any enterprise: legalize it. That manner, nobody else can be capable of thieving your brand or the ideas of your brands. In the event that they do, you'll be able to sue them in the courtroom legally. Legalizing your business entity is also a sure-shot way to earn credibility in the market because, in any case, all people want to be related to a felony enterprise in terms of sharing their money with them.

MAKE PROVISIONS FOR TAXATION

In case you are a legal, commercial enterprise entity, it's far obligatory that you have the taxation provisions on your commercial enterprise in place. This can assist you at the top of your monetary year when you eventually sit down right down to calculate the earnings or loss declaration for the yr. Plus, having proper taxation provision in the vicinity means that you will usually be transparent with the government bodies.

START A BUSINESS ACCOUNT

Begin a business account together with your financial institution. This enables you to maintain your enterprise transactions and your non-public financial transactions separate and offers your commercial enterprise the transparency it calls for with auditors. This may additionally help you stay out of hassle with the taxation government if all your cash is accounted for in preference to being reported as lacking.

GET ALL YOUR LICENSES AND PERMITS IN ORDER

A hydroponic commercial enterprise calls for special permission from the positive government. Make sure you get all your licenses and permits in the vicinity as this could reason trouble within the future and may result in your enterprise being close down for a quick while or even completely.

GET INSURED

Business coverage is extraordinarily vital and yet is either forgotten or omitted via most small and medium-sized businesses. These insurances help your enterprise in case there are any injuries, or unexpected circumstances that hit you within the destiny — matters that you ought to get insured for are standard legal responsibility coverage, business motors insurance, coverage for a facts breach, property insurance, coverage for disruption or temporary pause of enterprise and workers compensation insurance, in case of any mishaps. This may save you cash in the destiny and prevent you from going bankrupt.

GO DIGITAL

Virtual is where the action is, and in case you need to make your commercial enterprise live on and thrive, it's miles what you need to make your presence felt. Hydroponics is enormously new, and millennials are considering organic meals grown the proper manner. So, if you want to target millennials and businesses that focus on millennials, then digital is your great guess. Cross all out on social media, including Facebook, Instagram, and Twitter, and extra, and you will discover just the proper sort of customers in your merchandise. Now that you know all the fundamentals of starting a new hydroponic farming business, you could grow to be a fulfillment in the industry. It is time to start developing some environmental-friendly, organic, and surprisingly wholesome culmination and vegetables and start to give lower back to the surroundings in abundance.

STEPS TO CHOOSING THE BEST LOCATION FOR YOUR VEGETABLE GARDEN

Are you toying with the idea of developing a vegetable garden? Earlier than you launch this plan, you need to consider the location. Developing a garden isn't as easy as selecting a spot for your backyard and digging it out. There is much stuff you need to think about. If you aren't sure what you want to be seeking out to offer your lawn the fine shot, you got here to the right place. I'll inform you what you want to look for to discover the first-class spot in your garden.

Here is what you need to look for in a garden location:

FOLLOW THE SUN

Most vegetables preference complete daylight, which means that they may need access to the solar for at least six hours an afternoon. But the maximum plant is happier with greater. If you could find a region that gets full solar for 6 to 10 hours an afternoon, you found a niche; this is worth keeping underneath attention in your lawn. In case you don't have a place on your home that receives that sort of sunlight, do not forget clearing trees (if you have the option.)However, if you may clean bushes, then try and find an area that receives morning sun.

EVERYTHING NEEDS WATER

All of us need water. We can tot live without it. You want to maintain this in thoughts while searching out a vegetable lawn area. You'll want a vegetable garden area that is near water. If you should drag your water hose 20 feet to water the lawn, there is a good hazard; it will get left out. Make things as clean as you can to take care of your lawn by way of putting it close to water. Do not forget setting your garden near a water spigot. If that vicinity doesn't work well for other vegetable lawn area standards, bear in mind going for walks a water hose in your garden to make watering simpler. Also, when you have water nicely on your home, don't forget putting your garden close to the pump. That manner, you could look at once into the nicely for watering.

LET THE AIR FLOW

Your lawn needs to be in an area that can breathe. You don't need to plant it amongst a dense array of the different plants as it could be tough for air to circulate there. Alternatively, pick a vegetable garden region on the way to supply your garden ample space to respire. It desires to experience the wind. It may sound trivial. However, the right airflow can deter one-of-a-kind types of mildew and mold from growing in your plants. These illnesses can kill your garden, and they spread effortlessly. Airflow is one of the number one preventions for these diseases. If you fear your lawn getting too much wind, don't forget putting up a lawn wall. It has to maintain the wind from being harmful on your lawn while still giving it lots of air for respiratory.

CALL BEFORE YOU DIG

It is continually essential to name your local government before you start digging a garden, in particular in case you stay in city regions. In case you don't, you may, without problems, hit a water line or every other form of the buried utility line, pretty dangerous for the character digging! But, it can also motive problems in your family and your acquaintances as nicely if you accidentally hit a buried utility line. But more importantly, in case you hit an electric line underground while digging, it could be fatal. Make sure to realize what's under your capability vegetable garden region before you start growing it.

CONVENIENCE MATTERS

There are one of a kind reasons to begin a lawn. You could be developing for survival, growing for beauty, however regardless, you need to experience gardening on a few levels; otherwise, you wouldn't do it at all. That is why it's far advocated to put your lawn in a handy place. That way, you don't exit your way to get to it and experience it. Hold the lawn as close to your private home as you can for simplicity's sake. Additionally, if you need to position a patio to your garden to entertain in, it makes the area greater convenient and functional as properly.

NO TOXINS

The majority will not have to worry approximately this step within the vegetable garden region process. At the off danger, you're someone that could have this difficulty on their belongings; it is well worth the mention. In case you understand that substances inclusive of oil or lead paint have been dumped in selected vicinity on your private home, do not grow in the one's regions. Those substances can be in the ground and will show up on your food. It isn't safe or wholesome! With that in thoughts, avoid gardening in those places. Make sure that you area your garden as ways from those places as possible. If you are involved in approximately the safety of your soil, don't forget checking out your soil for contaminations.

AVOID FROST POCKETS

Frost's pockets can make gardening tough. We recognize that bloodless air sinks while heat air rises because cold air is denser than heat air. Because of this, cold air can find the bottom part of your garden and could relaxation there, causing frost pockets. Avoid planting in those regions due to the fact in case you plant a seedling in a frost pocket. It can be without difficulty killed. Maintain in mind wherein the frost wallet may be located. If you can cast off them out of your lawn, do it. If you may, you'll need to mark them to your lawn plan to keep away from planting in those locations.

EASY ACCESS

I already noted that it is good to pick out a handy vegetable garden area. You don't need to hike through the woods to get in your garden. As an alternative, region the lawn in which you may take a brief walk through your yard and experience it easily. Alongside the identical line, you want your vegetable garden location to be easily available as properly. If you may place your garden near a walkway, that could be best. A walkway makes it less difficult to stroll in your lawn whether or not or not it's to take care of it or entertain in it. Also, make sure you may maneuver a wheelbarrow easily to get on your garden. It wishes to be located where you could get garden supplies for your garden as really as feasible too.

CONSIDER HOA

In case you stay in a rural area, you may now not keep in mind in which you positioned your garden. It's far important to talk along with your landlord if you don't personal your home before planting a garden. But in case you live in an urban location, you'll want to check your HOA policies before planting a lawn. You don't want your lawn place to motive uproar inside the neighborhood. By planting your lawn according to your community guidelines, this can ensure that you may revel in gardening for future years without provoking any pals.

Chapter 15

Tips And Tricks To Growing Healthy
Herbs, Vegetables, And Fruits

TIPS FOR A HIGH-YIELD VEGETABLE GARDEN, EVEN WHEN YOU'RE TIGHT ON SPACE

Believe harvesting nearly half of a ton of tasty, stunning vegetables from a fifteen-by means of-20-foot plot, a hundred kilos of tomatoes from simply 100 rectangular feet, or 20 kilos of carrots from simply 24 rectangular ft. Yields like those are less complicated to obtain than you might imagine. The secret to awesome-effective gardening is taking the time now to devise strategies to be able to work for your garden. Right here are seven excessive-yield strategies gleaned from gardeners who have discovered to make the most of their garden space.

PLANT IN RAISED BEDS WITH RICH SOIL

Expert gardeners agree that building up the soil is the single maximum important thing in pumping up yields. A deep, organically rich soil encourages the increase of wholesome, substantial roots capable of reaching more nutrients and water. The result: more-lush, more-efficient boom above ground. The quickest way to get that deep layer of fertile soil is to make raised beds. Raised beds yield as much as four instances extra than the same amount of space planted in rows. That's due no longer best to their free, fertile soil but also green spacing. By way of the use of much less area for paths, you have got more room to grow plant life.

Raised beds save you time, too. One researcher tracked the time it took to plant and preserve a 30-through-30-foot garden planted in beds, and located that he needed to spend simply 27 hours in the garden from mid-may to mid-October. But he became able to harvest 1,900 pounds of clean veggies. That's a yr's delivery of food for three people from approximately three general days of work! How do you raise beds to keep a lot of time? Plant grow close sufficient collectively to crowd out competing weeds, so you spend much less time weeding. The near spacing additionally makes watering and harvesting more efficient.

ROUND OUT THE SOIL IN YOUR BEDS

The shape of your beds could make a distinction, too. Raised beds become more area-green through lightly rounding the soil to shape an arc. A rounded bed that is five toes extensive across its base, as an instance, may want to provide you with a 6-foot-extensive arc above it. That foot won't appear like much, however, multiply it through the duration of your bed, and you'll see that it can make a huge distinction in general planting place. In a 20-foot-long bed, as an instance, mounding the soil inside the middle increases your general planting region from 100 to 120 square feet. That's a 20% gain in planting area in a mattress that takes up an equal amount of floor space. Lettuce, spinach, and other veggies are the best plants for planting on the rims of a rounded mattress.

PLANT CROPS IN TRIANGLES INSTEAD OF ROWS

To get the most yields from every bed, be aware of how you arrange your plants. Avoid planting in rectangular patterns or rows. As an alternative, stagger the plant using planting in triangles. With the aid of doing so, you can fit 10 to fourteen% more plant life in each bed. Just be careful now not to area your plant too tightly. A few plant gainer reach their complete length — or yield — when crowded. As an example, while one researcher extended the spacing between romaine lettuces from 8 to 10 inches, the harvest weight consistent with the plant doubled. (Remember the fact that weight yield in line with the rectangular foot is more essential than the number of plants per rectangular foot.)Overly tight spacing also can strain plants, making them more at risk of sicknesses and bug assault.

GROW CLIMBING PLANTS TO CAPITALIZE ON SPACE

No matter how small your garden, you can develop extra via going vertical. Grow space-hungry vining crops—which include tomatoes, pole beans, peas, squash, melons, cukes, and so on—immediately up, supported by trellises, fences, cages, or stakes. Growing greens vertically also saves time. Harvest and renovation move quicker due to the fact you may see precisely wherein the fruits are. Fungal diseases are also less possible to have an effect on upward-bound plant sway to the stepped forward air circulates the foliage. Attempt growing vining plants on trellises alongside one side of raised beds, using robust cease posts with nylon mesh netting or string in between to offer a mountaineering surface. Tie the growing vines to the trellis. However, don't fear approximately securing heavy results. Even squash and melons will broaden thicker stems for guide.

PICK COMPATIBLE PAIRINGS

Interpolating well-suited vegetation saves space, too. Bear in mind the conventional local American mixture, the "3 sisters:" corn, beans, and squash. Robust cornstalks aid the pole beans, even as squash grows freely at the floor underneath, shading out competing weeds. Other well-suited combinations encompass tomatoes, basil, and onions; leaf lettuce and peas or brassicas; carrots, onions, and radishes; and beets and celery.

TIME YOUR CROPS CAREFULLY

Succession planting allows you to grow more than one crop in a given area over the direction of a growing season. That way, many gardeners can harvest three or even four vegetation from a single vicinity. As an instance, comply with an early crop of leaf lettuce with a fast-maturing corn, after which develop greater greens or overwintered garlic — all inside a single growing season. To get the most from your succession plantings:

- **Use transplants.** A transplant is already a month or so old while you plant it, and matures that **an awful lot** faster than a seed sown without delay within the garden.

- Pick fast-maturing types.

- **Fill up the soil** with a ¼-to-½-inch layer of compost (about two cubic ft in step with one hundred rectangular toes) whenever you replant. Work it into the pinnacle a few inches of soil.

STRETCH YOUR SEASON BY COVERING THE BEDS

Adding a few weeks to each stop of the growing season should buy you sufficient time to develop some other succession crop yet — say a planting of leaf lettuce, kale, or turnips — or to harvest extra give up-of-the-season tomatoes. To get those greater weeks of production, you want to keep the air around your vegetation heat (even when the weather is cold) by way of the use of mulches, cloches, row covers, or bloodless frames. Or give warmth-loving vegetation (inclusive of melons, peppers, and eggplants) an additional-early begin in the spring using the use of "blankets" — one to heat the air and one to warm the soil. About six to 8 weeks earlier than the closing frost date, preheat cold soil via covering it with both infrared-transmitting (IRT) mulch and black plastic so that one can absorb warmness. Then, cowl the mattress with a slitted, clear plastic tunnel. While the soil temperature reaches 65 to 70 tiers Fahrenheit, set out plant and cowl the black plastic mulch with straw to preserve it from trapping too much heat. Take away the clean plastic tunnel when the air temperature warms, and all chance of frost has passed. Install it once more at the give up of the season while temperatures cool.

Tips And Tricks For Building Your Own Hydroponic Garden

- recognize what tools you need and why

- recognize the dietary requirements of your plant life

- recognize the light/photoperiod requirements of your flora

- Use an expert 3 part hydroponic vitamins product

- Do now not use additional nutrient additives your first time

- Have a written plan/feeding time table earlier than you start

- Have all the vital tools and vitamins before you begin

- lawn indoors when it's far fifty five*F or much less outside (or use AC)

- hold the ballast in your lights in a different room

- take a look at and regulate your nutrient reservoir solution every day

- minimize light exposure on your nutrient answer

- Have an additional reservoir of pure water watching for your next nutrient trade

- exchange your water and vitamins absolutely every two weeks

- Use a digital timer to govern your darkish period

- hold your dark period completely dark and un-interrupted

- clean and sterilize your system among plants

- Quarantine new vegetation for two weeks before adding on your garden

- Do not go to your garden after touring every other lawn or being exterior

- Do now not permit pets on your lawn

- go to your garden after a bath and a fresh change of garments

- Make any site visitors on your lawn comply with these identical regulations

- placed a display screen or filter out over your air consumption and exhaust (if outside)

Chapter 16

Mistakes Of Your Hydroponic Garden
Myths And Mistakes To Avoid

COMMON MISTAKES MADE IN HYDROPONIC GARDENS

In case you're just beginning out along with your hydroponic lawn, you need to take things slow and easy. One mistake can ruin all the development you've made to your growth. As an alternative, make an effort to understand what your plant expects from you and the situations they want. Many problems can get up in a hydroponic lawn, but right here are the five maximum-commonplace errors a hydro gardener can make:

MISTAKE 1 – IGNORING PH LEVELS

The most treasured size for your hydroponic system is its pH stage. For the maximum component, your plant exists nearly absolutely way to a nutrient answer. If that answer is too alkaline or too acidic, your plant will enjoy nutrient deficiencies or certainly die. Get yourself a pinnacle-notch pH meter and monitor the ranges at least as soon as a day. If it slides in one direction or any other, take instantaneous steps to bring it returned into the balance your plant want. An off-kilter pH degree is one of the maximum commonplace reasons for plant die-offs in a hydroponic gadget. It's particularly important to display pH tiers because all your plant stays within the equal nutrient solution – in case your pH is awful for one plant, all of your plant life may want to suffer!

MISTAKE 2 – BUYING CHEAP, INCORRECT OR NOT ENOUGH LIGHTING

Investing within the proper lights can make or wreck your hydroponic lawn! If you purchase too little, your plants will go through. If you buy the incorrect type of bulb in your plant, they gained growth. In case you opt to buy the most inexpensive bulbs, they will not perform. Lights are one of the maximum critical investments you'll make as a hydroponic grower, so are searching for out the best for your crop! This indicates you need to research the form of mild your plant will want due to the fact one-of-a-kind bulbs positioned out one-of-a-kind power kinds. Also, don't assume your plant to thrive if they're set after a window. That mild is frequently now not strong sufficient to gasoline the full of life boom you anticipate from a hydroponic plant.

MISTAKE 3 – USING THE WRONG PLANT FOOD

It may be tempting to buy a sack of fertilizer from your neighborhood lawn middle for use to your hydroponic device. After all, it's all approximately turning in nutrients. No longer so! Conventional fertilizer might not dilute absolutely through your machine. Likewise, it can clog drains and tubes. As a substitute, invest in fertilizer designed for hydroponic structures. Hydroponic fertilizer that is to be had as liquids or granules meets the growing necessities you need in a soil-much less or soil-mild lawn by imparting extra vitamins your plant may in any other case leave out.

MISTAKE 4 – NOT FOCUSING ON SANITATION

Don't permit your hydroponic garden region to come to be a garbage bin. Your sanitation habits will have a major impact on the fitness of your plant life and your complete hydroponic gadget.

Some simple cleansing desires that you should cope with:

- retaining floors easy and dry
- Sterilizing and cleaning machine device
- Sterilizing and cleaning tools
- Sterilizing and cleaning bins
- putting off plant waste
- Without the right sanitation, you can spread plant ailment or provide pests with hiding places and sustenance.

MISTAKE 5 – OPTING NOT TO LEARN

Current hydroponic structures were around for the reason that the early 20th century, and in that time, quite a few data and guidance have been made available. College guides are taught on it. Hundreds of books are available. You could even find loads hydroponic developing records here on the more secure® logo with ordinary updates in our Articles section. In short, don't cross it alone! Examine up and make a plan in your hydroponic lawn. Speak to other hydroponic gardeners and proportion ideas. The greater you realize before putting in your garden, the better off you'll be by the time you're ready to reap.

How To Avoid Common Mistakes In Hydroponics?

While growing hydroponic vegetation, the maximum of the growers devote the equal common mistakes which smash their complete garden. With proper studies and planning, you may avoid several such common mistakes. One of the most important errors growers commonly devote is they begin growing hydroponics plants while not having any basic expertise about how to grow and appearance after hydroponically grown plant life. Earlier than you start your hydroponic garden, take a look at our tale that offers you confidence in hydroponic development! One commonplace mistake most of the gardeners commit is to no longer offer enough air movement inside their hydroponic garden. Air motion is critical to plant' respiration because it offers clean air to your leaf area. The air to your develop room has to incorporate sufficient oxygen, CO2, but it must no longer comprise molecules of commercial pollution, particulates, and other airborne particles. Proper ventilation is vital to get larger yields in hydroponic gardening; however, you can not throw a fan to your hydroponic grow room. You need to put a proper length fan as hydroponics enthusiasts are a vital part of your indoor lawn set up and help to manage airflow, warmness, and different environmental conditions. If you are the usage of concealed develop lights, ventilation becomes even greater vital due to the amount of heat those lights produce. Constantly recollect to maintain the fan in consistent motion, and it needs to now not blow without delay at the plant as this can reason dehydration.

Hydroponics plant life flourishes in easy and well-maintained surroundings, so you ought to clear all the debris inclusive of fallen leaves, dirt, and other substances that could entice and breed illnesses. You want to preserve your grow room dry to keep away from any form of fungal infestation. Do no longer smoke, eat, or permit pets near the vegetation as those can offer harm to your plant. To keep away from these not unusual mistakes on your hydroponic garden, you need to pay near interest for your plant life each day to ensure that your garden is jogging easily. Every time you go to your lawn, consider checking your pump structures, reservoirs, water degrees, pH, nutrients, lights, timers, and plants.

Conclusion

As you could see, there are some things you want to hold a watch on or keep in mind while putting in a hydroponic gadget. With the fundamentals of your water and vitamins, the effect of lighting, and ventilation, you may cover nearly everything. A number of this will rely upon your development space, and when you have to get admission to external windows or it's far sealed off, and you're utterly reliant on developing lights. As soon as you have got these simple fundamentals beneath manipulate, you're in a role to take on any hydroponic system due to the fact the equal basic regulations could be the same. Once you examine the basics, you could fast extend any gadget or construct a bigger one from scratch. Quite a few, the amusing is in discovering new recommendations and techniques, but those fundamentals will in no way change.